Sita's Introspection

In Uttara Ramayana

Bhagya Shree Nadamala

Ukiyoto Publishing

To my Teachers at
Madras Christian College, Chennai
Sri Venkateswara University, Tirupati
Indian Institute of Technology Patna

Author's Note

As a part of my Doctoral research on Gender Studies at Indian Institute of Technology Patna, I have gone through extensive research and a long biographical journey with Sita Devi of Valmiki's Ramayana. This journey not just allowed me to peep into Sita's world but made me a companion of her achievements and travails. In this book, I attempted to voice Sita Devi's inner feelings in Uttara kanda of Ramayana as "Sita's Introspection in Uttara Ramayana".

How did Sita Devi react when her people rejected her after being abducted by Ravana, how did she being pregnant feel when her husband Rama left her alone in the perilous forest, how did she bring up her children as great warriors, and how did she feel when her husband asked her to prove chastity in front of public and children? I tried to turn Sita Devi's every inner feeling into words in this book.

The book starts at Ayodhya's Durbar Hall with Rama's coronation and ends at the same Durbar Hall with Sita Devi's reunion with her mother, Bhudevi. Entire text runs between these two incidents. I am sure readers shall feel pride, joy, dignity, shock, courage, humility, hope, obedience, brave, honour, sympathy, and empathy at every moment of Sita's life.

I entered the Durbar hall of our Ayodhya kingdom with Rama. Garlands of mango leaves and exotic flowers collected from the surrounding hamlets are hanging with poise. The flowers are arranged and aligned in different styles and patterns, setting the hall in a festive ambience. The fresh aroma generated from the wide-ranging flowers is providing an instant refreshment to my mind. My heart is filled with joy witnessing the varied levels of happiness on everyone's countenances and pride in their eyes.

Amidst thousands of Ayodhyians, rishis and common people, dancers and musicians, demi-gods and family members, amidst the chanting of mantras, the victory trumpet sounds, Rama-nama-japam, Sage Vasishta crowned my dear Lord Rama as the King of Ayodhya Kingdom and me as Ayodhya's Queen, in the presence of panchamahabhuta. The common public, rishis, mother-in-laws Kousalya, Sumitra, and Kaikeyi, and brother-in-laws Lakshmana, Bharata, and Shatrugna, all are delighted to see their beloved Ramachandra's grand and colourful coronation.

The moment they have been waiting for has come, as the tumultuous days of fourteen years have passed without the rule of a king. Bharata denied kingship and placed Rama's sandals on the throne. Those were the days with neither king nor glory. I cannot even imagine Ayodhya, an ever-flourishing state with blissful people, happy mothers, playful kids, adequate rains, and green fields, was rather a dreary and sombre place. I cannot even think more of Ayodhya's dark and gloomy picture.

With the return of former glory, everyone is in a joyous state. I am delighted to find the lost joy in the faces of young and old men and women. Rama is taking the oath as a King with pride, "I promise to ensure people's interest as my own and shall place people's opinion before my own. I promise to rule without paying attention to my personal interests and likes." The whole congregation is reverberating with Rama-naamam "Jai Sree Ram! Jai Jai Sree Ram! Jai Sree Ram! Jai Jai Sree Ram!"

Rama seems to be in a meditative state, probably thinking about how to rule the kingdom effectively and efficiently, how to lead by following and preaching dharma, and how to rule righteously, bestowing happiness and prosperity. His mind appears to be occupied with the dream of making Ayodhya an ideal kingdom. He might also be perplexed about the loss of his dear father Dasharath Maharaja. The latter would have had enormous satisfaction and completeness on seeing Rama being coronated as Ayodhya's King, his long-term dream.

As people are enjoying watching the coronation and cherishing the joyous moments and Rama is engrossed in his own thoughts on building a faultless kingdom; a flow of uncontrollable thoughts is gushing into my mind. Along with these thoughts, some sense of gloom attached to despondency is sickening me. It feels as if I am reliving the fourteen years again.

Those were the years of peaceful aesthetic life and the years of Kshatriya conflict, the years of surprises and dangers, the years of unpredictability and hopelessness, the years of unknown destiny, and the years of falling self-trust and endless sacrifices. Even though troubles beckoned me, especially in the forest, I did not feel so burdened as we faced the problems together. There is no safest place in the world other than being beside my dear Rama. Oh! No. I do not want to even think about the last year at the Dashagriva Lanka.

I have learnt and unlearnt many aspects of life. This one long year in Lanka has been my best teacher. I learnt how to self-protect myself, how to be fearless, how to stand unaffected by baseless demands, how to be hopeful of the future, how to be optimistic, and how to be self-motivated. Even though I relished every moment, it felt as if I was alone in this vast universe. Maybe my Rama's absence was worrying me a lot. Not even one present here can understand my situation. I fought all alone. But why am I dooming into the uncolourful past on the day of coronation? These thoughts never struck me so hard before; why am I glooming on this day of glory?

***

We started our adventurous journey as the new King and Queen by taking blessings from the head of the Ikshvaku dynasty, Surya Bhagavan, and all the elders. Seeing myself adorned with a complete set of precious jewels gave me a completely new feeling. It made me realize that I have lost the habit of decorating myself. I thought that aranyavasam had turned me old. But no, I was wrong. I am looking even more beautiful today. As I am self-adoring myself, I was also thinking if it was only me feeling odd at myself. I was taken aback when Rama said, "Sita, as I see you embellished with all the exquisite jewels, even after many years, my Sita when I was bringing her to Ayodhya from Mithila is flickering across my mind. I am still experiencing the same sense of innocence in your eyes, the unflinching smile of courage, the eternal feeling of tranquillity on your forehead, and the same air of pride in your eyebrows. Your presence in this form is so mesmerizing that it makes me forget our difficulties."

Rama and I were nostalgic together. We spent the rest of the night engaging in reposeful contemplation. Our talks were of no bounds. I am enjoying this late-night discussion; I am enjoying the way we are speaking our hearts out. We travelled all the worlds in our imaginary conversation. I was amazed and a bit shocked to see Rama, a Surya Vamshi marking a Chandra bimbam beneath my bindi, right between my two eyebrows. Exhausted after a long and busy day, I could not control my sleep. While I was about to doze off, I heard a loud, sharp bell signalling Rama's presence at the court. Rama has to look after his new responsibility. As an understanding wife, I cannot ask him to be by my side always. Beyond me, he has to look after the concerns of his citizens. He has already gone through extreme suffering and excruciating pain while tracing me and destroying Ravana Lanka. It would be foolish to ask him to spend more time with me. Ruminating on these thoughts, I fell asleep.

***

How do you feel when you get some good news as soon as you wake up? Wouldn't you be thrilled to start the day with such a piece of fantastic news? And what could be the most wonderful news a married woman can get? What could be that news which makes a married woman extra special? Yes, you have guessed it right.

The news that I am conceived gives me utmost pleasure at this time. I am going to be a mother, and there's one more life breathing inside me. Listening to what I speak gives me a completely different feel, which is inexpressible, the feel that only mothers can relate to. Now our to-be-born child would continue the legacy of the reputed Ikshvaku dynasty and is to become the prince of Ayodhya.

I should take enough care to raise my child equal to his father in terms of astraprayogam, sarvendriyanigraham, patience, and dharma. All of these would double my responsibility. It's not easy to raise a king's son. Every eye in the nook and corner would be scrutinizing the prince's talent, constantly comparing him with his father. These eyes would even decide if the prince is capable enough to become Ayodhya's king.

My thoughts have travelled way before time. Sooner the news is spread from the four walls to the length and breadth of Ayodhya and beyond the fort walls. Just the announcement has brought festivity to the Durbar palace. People are happy to witness Ayodhya in prosperity. While everyone else's joy was boundless, Rama's joy was on a completely different level. I can see some new spark in his eyes and overwhelming ecstasy while he is caressing me. He often says, "Sita, this is perhaps the most immeasurable gift that you have given me and our kingdom. I am out of words and do not have anything equivalent in return. No present can be as high as this."

"My Lord, you are the greatest gift that I got in my life. For me, this is the highest. Just being by your side gives me immense joy. This is why I argued with you and came along to the aranyavasam, even though you warned me of the forest's unknown dangers. I cannot even imagine spending the days without you here at Ayodhya."

And as months passed, the talks about the most auspicious event for anyone expecting a child started circulating.

***

My mothers-in-law are engrossed in discussing the auspicious date and timing for performing my sreemantham. Usually, maternal parents take responsibility for performing this ritual. It is the first event that the maternal side of the family loves performing for their daughter. My father, King Janak of Mithila kingdom, has come to Ayodhya this morning. It has been a long time since I saw and spoke with my father.

In my childhood, I spent many memorable days discussing aspects ranging from home to public ruling. We both set an end to every day by analyzing the general rule of that day, the problems to resolve, and the ways to develop Mithila into a flourishing state. Our bonding grew more robust with the days. Though I was found by King Janak while ploughing the field for a yagna, he never showed any biasness towards me. Moreover, he treated me just like my sister Urmila. King Janak, Queen Sunaina, my sister Urmila and I discuss public affairs, which are quite unusual in most of the ruling states as women were not considered capable enough to discuss public issues.

My father's presence at Ayodhya makes me nostalgic about my life before marriage. I was a young daughter helping my father. My swayamvar lasted for several days, with each prince from different parts of the princely states trying their best to string the Shivadhanassu, eligibility for my hand in marriage. Every day I get decked up and stand with a garland in my hand, but none of the princes strung the bow. Until my dear Rama came, he broke it smoothly and effortlessly while trying to string it. I have found my man. We have then exchanged garlands.

For the first time, I trusted a man other than my father. I knotted my little finger with his and walked around the holy fire. It felt like I was leaving my father's hands permanently. My father's arrival today also brought happiness alongside many childhood memories and marriage recollections. I went to the Durbar hall to receive him and took his blessings. But it feels like my father did not come to see me, alone.

He called my mothers-in-law Kausalya, Sumitra, Kaikeyi, and Rama's brothers Lakshmana, Bharata, and Shatrugna were present.

Addressing Kausalya, King Janak said, "I cannot put my feelings in words how happy I am after listening to the good news. After seeing my dear Sita after so many years, my joy is of no bounds. The news that I will soon become a grandfather to Sita's children makes me complete."

My father would not come from Mithila just to express his happiness. Does he have something else to tell? He would definitely have something to offer, but why is my father not discussing it? As I was ruminating on my own thoughts, my father asked something to Kausalya. She replied, "Yes, I know the ritual of the maternal side performing the first function after their daughter's marriage. You do not even need to ask about this. Sita is your daughter first, and then ours. You have the right to take her home for importantoccasions like these." Now I understand the purpose behind my father's arrival, but nearly after a year of staying away from my dear Rama, I do not wish to go home, leaving Rama behind. Without any second thought, I went to my father and said, "My dear father, I have a request for you. I am happy that you have come all the way from Mithila to Ayodhya. You all know how much I suffered over the past year. I have gone through the worst days of my life in Lanka. Those days made me strong, but I was potentially weak without Rama by my side. It was then that I decided never to leave Rama. You all have decided to send me with my father Janak. I am grateful for that, but dear father, please let me stay by my husband's side here at Ayodhya, and I am sure that my mothers-in-law would perform best sreemantham for me."

I am eagerly waiting for my father's response, looking keenly into his eyes. "As you like Sita, you do not need to request me like this. Be at whatsoever place that makes you happy." These words from my father sounded so musically sweet to me. I took a deep breath and blessings from my father before leaving. He blessed me, and it felt surreal when he added my soul beating inside to the list and took leave. I rushed towards Rama and held his hands with so much happiness.

***

Days passed by spending most of the time daydreaming by looking at the beautiful nest right outside my window, on a tree. It's so fascinating that initially when I saw it was just a mother bird hatching its eggs. I saw her most of the time sitting on the eggs, protecting her unborn babies from some cruel birds and snakes trying to snatch those eggs away. Sometimes I see her almost all day, sitting over there, calmly, and her eyes everywhere on her enemies. I adore the way she protects her babies. Apart from the amusing scenic beauty, she sets in, I find her very inspiring, allowing me to self-assess myself.

This has been my routine for most of the days. But one day, as I am spending my time contemplating so many happy thoughts, a newly hung picture at Ayodhya palace stuck my attention. It was so captivating. Amidst all the hustle and bustle of the court, and the endless noises of the workers, and people, seeing that picture is so relaxing. It's my husband and me at an ashram during the aranyavasam. I still remember the moment clearly.

This picture is the next most relaxing, apart from the sight of the mother bird. The soothing noises of nature, life away from the chaotic city, all of this flashed before my eyes at once. Without thinking any second thought, which is usually against my nature. I ran to my Rama and asked my wish, "Rama! I wish to go near the Ganga River. I also wish to visit various rishi's hermitages and seek blessings."

Rama was taken aback after knowing my decision to spend my time at ashrams, aware of the innumerable problems we have faced over there for years. "Sita, why do you even need to go there all alone? If you want, I can ask the ascetics to come to Ayodhya and bless us." But I somehow convinced my dear Rama to allow on a short trip to the ashrams, which is an arduous task. When I saw the picture hanging on the wall, I was nervous to ask Lord Rama about his decision. And as soon as he accepted, I should be elated that he accepted but now, I do not understand why my heart is swinging forth and back with endless thoughts. Every thought that brought me happiness to visit hermitages, now those very thoughts of leaving Rama are sickening me. This time some unknown pain is inflicting me. I cannot imagine being away from my Rama in my dreams.

****

I woke up to get ready. For the first time after many days, I witnessed the nest with a difference. The mother bird never leaves her children and is always found having an eye on the prey. But, today, the nest had only three eggs, with the mother missing. My heart crumbled as soon as I witnessed this sight and searched for the missing mother, but all my searches were in vain. I am trying to locate but failed to, even amidst innumerable glances. With a dissatisfied heart, I started getting ready with the jewellery, but not as finest as I usually do.

The second surprise in a row has found its way. Rama has the habit of waking up early in the morning to perform Surya Namaskar. But today when I went to bid adieu, I still found him sleeping, which is unnatural. I checked twice by touching his feet and waited for some time to see if he woke up, but he did not. Disappointed that I was leaving without informing my dear Rama, I took my last blessings and left.

Lakshmana was waiting to drop me off.

"Lakshmana, who asked you to drop me at the ashram?" I asked Lakshmana.

Without lifting his head, he said, "Rama."

We started the journey to the ashram on a horse cart. As I travelled, the divide between the kingdom and the forest was quite visible. The fresh air from the deep, dense forests is refreshing, the chirping sounds of birds are welcoming, and the animals are waiting on either side of the road to cross the path, but Lakshmana seems unnatural.

Without any second thought, I can tell that he is not natural from the experience of our stay in the forest for over thirteen years. He is very active, loves to talk and gets us engaged with beautiful descriptions of the scenery while travelling, but today I didn't listen to him speak a word at least. I am just enjoying my own company. He neither looked around at nature nor spoke a word. But all of a sudden, Lakshmana stopped the cart, and we got down.

My eyes searched for the ashram. But I didn't find any hermitage nearby. Out of curiosity, I asked Lakshmana, "What is this? Did we miss the route?"

"Sita Mata, forests usually do not have any routes", said Lakshmana with sorrow voice.

"Lakshmana! Why is your face so dull? Are you not happy with me going for the ashram visit? Or are you unhappy because I asked for an ashram visit that your brother does not like?"

By nodding his head, "Sita Mata, how can I be happy thinking about your difficulties."

"Lakshmana, this aranyavasam, I will just be there for a few days and not my entire life."

"O! Sita Mata! How can I tell you, In Ayodhya, just because one commoner questioned your purity, Rama has ordered to leave you in the forest permanently to maintain the kingdom's dignity", he said, crying.

"Lakshmana! Where is dharma? Am I that sinful? If Rama has called me and informed me about the situation and not even asked, ordered me to go to the forest or leave the forest, I am even ready to jump into the fire again. Ever since we returned from the forest, I never thought about leaving, Rama and I gave utmost importance to Sree Rama Seva. Is this the respect I deserve for being chaste and proving my chastity through agnipariksha? Did you people bring me to Ayodhya just to leave me in the forest like this? Why this spoilt life? Everything would be good and right if I surrender myself to Ganga", I said with most profound sorrow.

"Sita Mata! Promise on me, please don't do that", wept Lakshmana.

"When I don't get a chance to see my Rama and be with him, what's the purpose of this life?" I spoke.

"Sita Mata, please spare your life at least for the souls growing in your womb", requested Lakshmana.

"If I am thrown away like this, will my kids be accepted? How can I show my face to the world?" I wept.

"Sita Mata! Please have patience and show the world that the ideals of satya and dharma will win at any cost. Mata! Do you think Rama is happy leaving you? Even Rama is so sad. Do you think he could live without you?"

"Yes, Lakshmana, you are right. I spoke ill about Rama out of grief. Just ignore it. I am born for troubles."

But Lakshmana is also equally helpless. He is standing between two things. On the one hand is Ramagna, which he cannot cross; on the other hand, I am standing in the middle of the forest. He finds it hard to leave me here. He stands unopposed to his father-like-brother and is helpless to his mother-like-sister-in-law. With a high level of contempt and a heavy heart, Lakshmana left the forest.

***

Now again, I stand here in the same position that I was in one year ago. Then, Ashoka vanam was an unknown land, unknown people, and unknown destiny. Nobody was familiar, not even my future. Will my Rama know where I am? Will he kill the ten-headed Ravana and rescue me? This is a known land, known people, with whom I spent nearly 14 years. But in this land, I was sent by Rama, and there is no enemy to defeat. But it is the same question in another form. Will my Rama come to take me back? How does this act of blame upon me even vanish? How long is this going to last? I have gone through a fire ordeal for being at Ravana's place, not the palace. Even after the test that usually no woman would like to get tested against, the test has become of no value now. What else should I even do to remove this black mark upon me? Will another fire ordeal vanish the mark? As a king, yes, I agree with Rama's oath that he promised to put people's interests before his personal interest. Yes, he did a kingly duty, and as people did not witness the fire ordeal, they spoke ill about me.

Now, if I do another ordeal, and if people who could not witness it suspect my chastity, should I do it for them again? Will this ever end? The thought that I was being doubted of chastity once again is making me sick. Now, as I reflect, I could draw a line between the unnatural and unusual things, the unnatural disappearance of the bird on her three hatched eggs, and Rama's unusual act of sleep. Maybe the burden of leaving me without informing has made him hard to even look at me. Whom should I blame? Should I blame my birth? Mother. Mother goddess, out of this grief, I could not hold back my tears and fell flat on the ground.

Suddenly, the frightening apparition of Lord Rama's suffering alerted me. He seems so unstable and is in motion. His throne is also displaced completely and appears to fall straight on Rama. The trees are swinging and uprooting, heavy rocks from the nearby mountains are rolling down with great force, and the sky is lit with heavy thundering sounds and lightning. Amidst this havoc, I saw the rise of my mother in a complete rage. Her eyes are fiery red, her hair appears to be dancing to the rhythm of Lord Shiva, and the trident in her hands seems to be showcasing her inner rage. I went crawling on the ground as fast as I could, held her legs, and requested, "Mother, I can bear an endless amount of pain inflicted upon me with ease, but I cannot bear a small pain inflicted upon my dear husband, Rama. Please calm down."

"Rama? What Rama? He is the one who sent a pregnant wife to the forest, a stone-hearted person. He is a ruthless person who has put a lot of trouble for his own wife. Still, you are crying for Rama."

"Mother, since I am your daughter, you have the right to shout at me, whatever you want. But if you blame my dear Rama in front of me, I cannot tolerate it."

"Sita, seeing your plight, did you even imagine how much I am suffering? You married Rama, then went to forests, became friends with problems, even after all these many problems that Rama…"

"Mother, he is Sitamanobhirama. Even if I am in the forest, or I get stranded in the ocean, I would overflow with undefined happiness just by hearing Rama's name. Mother, what do you know? I cannot tolerate if anyone blames my Rama."

"Sita! Sita! You are pregnant. Why be in trouble? Please come with me. My little Sita."

"Mother, for those grieving in suffocation, there is no better place in this world than a mother's hug. But mother, I cannot come now."

"Why?" asked my mother, Bhudevi.

"Mother, bearing blame and coming to my mother's home will not be respectful to me. For being born in your womb, for stepping into Raghuvamsham and holding Rama's hand, I will hand him his own imprint and come. Please forgive me, mother."

"This is the problem if we give birth to a girl child, face your own karma."

I was about to reply, but she slowly disappeared into the air. Not just for me, but for any married daughter, as soon as she knows that she has a problem in her in-law's home, a mother would be the first one to offer help, and my mother is no excuse.

Unable to bear the trouble, she came not just to offer solace with her words but also to take me along with her. She is right from her perspective; no mother wants her daughter's married life to be full of problems. They just cannot bear it. She would have come with the hope that I would go with her. But I know I have disappointed her with my decision. This is not the right time to go to my mother's home. I should clean myself of the blame; I should complete my responsibility as a wife and mother by giving my dear Rama his children.

***

The forest also looks much more confusing. The same forest I found very appealing, which took me back to good old memories, now appears very dry and clueless. Flowers were blooming with very fresh dew drops on them covered like silver enamel, now appearing dried due to constant heat outside. The trees were swinging effortlessly in the morning, which felt like a flower rain outside. Now not even a tree branch seems to be moving, not just the tree; the world appears to stand still. It seems that the world is also grieving my pain.

The second thought that came rushing into my mind, due to which I am self-questioning myself, is, am I the only one feeling this way? I heard from many people in Ayodhya that nature reflects our moods. I think I am turning philosophic these days. In Mithila, as a kid, my major routine was to discuss with my father the existing problems and the aspects of development. The call for the swayamvar changed our discussions from state matters to conversing on the apt groom for me. Every day, some prince from far off land would try to string the bow and fails. At night, we at length discuss the stories attached to that groom; who is he? Did he do something interesting in his state? We neither judged any groom nor criticized him. We only discussed the development schemes he implemented, so we could also try them in our state. All of these happened for months and later ended with Rama's successful lifting of the bow. And after stepping into my in-law's house, I initially felt pressured to be a good daughter-in-law and an ideal wife to a purushottama like Rama. All my thoughts were circulating only in and around Ayodhya. But as soon as Lakshmana left me here, my mind looks pretty unnatural. The assortment of thoughts started to hover around. My mind is heavy with these otherwise useless thoughts, and physically, I also appear weak due to the scorching heat. In this otherwise stable world, I am walking aimlessly between the trees with heavy tears in my eyes.

On the one hand, I am carrying the pain that my Sree Rama, my husband, sent me to this uninhabited wilderness; on the other hand, lives the pain that I have rejected my mother's wish to take me back home. I am not able to find a way. I feel weak due to the physical pressure on the womb. I need to live for the souls breathing inside me. Though I said to Lakshmana that I would die, I regret saying that as human life is very much valuable, and one should live to their purpose of birth. My Rama's blood is inside my womb. They should be feeling hungry as well, and I need to find some shed-like place to rest for some time, have water, and grab some fruits available in the forest. But I could not see at least one person in this vast forest. Yes, why would people roam in the woods? This land is located far from Ayodhya and near ashramas. Why would anyone be seen here? I am out of the world. I have restarted walking to find some shelter in this scorching heat.

***

I heard a voice, and much to my surprise, someone was calling me by my name. Who would know me in this vast jungle? How could anyone know me in this place, far away from Ayodhya? Maybe some rishi from those years of stay in the forest would have recognized me. With so much speculation, I turned behind. One old sage was walking toward me. I could see intense apprehension in his eyes, and in a shivering tone, he spoke, "Mother, you are pregnant and without even knowing about the forest, what is this, what is this adventure."

"Where is the right direction? And what is the need to even think about direction? My life has become directionless. Where is the way to live my life by keeping my head up?"

"Please cool down, mother. With my cognitive power, I understood everything. I am Valmiki, who wrote your Sitaramacharitham in Ramayana form. My birth is meaningful and complete with your darshan. Please come to my hermitage and make us grateful."

"Mahatma, greetings. If you give residence to a blamed person like me, your hermitage's reputation will ruin. If people come to know that a black-marked person like me, whom Rama has thrown outside the Ayodhya Kingdom, is finding shelter in your reputable hermitage, your hermitage people shall also despise me. Hence, please forgive me. Thank you for offering residence at your place. But even if I wish to come, I am tied harder with the rope called blame."

"What a big word you spoke. Why do you get blamed? You are adishakti, jaganmata, adilakshmi. I know your greatness, Sita Mata. Please come to my hermitage where Rama-nama-japam is always done. Just look at the people and our respect toward your ideals."

"Munindra, you have appeared like a God who brought me to the shore from this disastrous ocean. You appeared like a gallon of water in the desert. You appeared like a helping hand in times of trouble, like an umbrella in the rain and a fresh breeze in hot summer. At once, I will come to your ashram and purify my birth. But before that, I have one request for you. I wish to live a life of anonymity. None should know my name. I shall start a new life in disguise. Please bless me."

"How can there be a naming deficit to you? People offer prayers to you in different names. You can be in the hermitage as Loka Pavani."

I know Valmiki would be quite shocked after listening to my request to change my name. I have two reasons for this. I do not want people to give special attention to me. Knowing that I am their Sita would cause unnecessary fuss amongst themselves and would lead to disturbance in their everyday lifestyle. Everybody will start talking about me, putting their regular work aside, which is not good. Beyond all that, I would get special attention, which I detest.

And the second reason is that if they know I am Sita, besides talking about me, they would also judge Rama and speak so many things offensive to him which is hard to hear as a wife. I understand his decision. Likewise, not everyone would have the same sense of understanding. Out of anger, they would definitely keep gushing about-if Rama would ever accept me, will Rama bring a new queen, what will be my future, and many more. I know that my thoughts have travelled beyond anyone can guess. I should stop here. I have made the right decision to change my name. Deeply immersed in my thoughts, I did not pay attention to the nature around me, which I usually do. Within minutes we arrived at Valmiki's ashram. This place, right at the first sight, gives me some peace after the hoax of violence that the weather and the proceeding conversation with my mother. The sight of beautiful peacocks outside, which had just opened their feathers completely and are dancing to the natural music made by different birds outside, felt like a warm welcome to me. This place started to feel divine. Maharshi introduced me to the people, rishis, and so many children learning under rishis. I am introduced to all of them as Loka Pavani.

***

Usually, getting adjusted to a place takes some days or a month at least. If a queen is sent to the forest for the first time, she would face so many difficulties. The customs and traditions stand completely varied. The place itself might not have all the facilities that the royal palace has got, lifestyle is different. It would be a completely new experience for them. But the experience of already living in the forest for fourteen years is helping me now. I did not take much time to get accustomed to people over here. This place is occupied by brahmins and their children engrossed in studying and learning the Vedic texts.

My first sleep here at the ashram went effortlessly. I did not take much time to sleep because being tired physically and mentally sidelined my thoughts. And today, I did not wake up with my people around but rather with two sounds. Firstly, the chirping sounds of birds and then the place is vibrated with Rama-nama chanting. It sounds so magical, heavenly and holy to wake up with these chanting mantras. It's so pleasant to wake up in nature's lap with the fresh breeze touching my face. It's as if my mother kissed me.

My first sight as soon as I wake up is generally Rama. But today, one pretty white rabbit hopping this side to that side along with his mother caught my sight. If I am not wrong, he would have been born just days before as he is still limping. It even felt absurd as I couldn't perform padhaseva to my dear Rama. This is usually the first activity that I would start my day with. My first worship would go to my husband. But today, as Rama is not beside me, I started the day by imagining my Rama's presence, and I took his blessings.

In the hermitage, early morning appears much like mid-day. All people are busy with their own chores. The brahmin kids seated around Valmiki Maharshi are listening to his teachings carefully. I had been observing them for some minutes, yet they did not turn their heads. It shows the respect they are showing towards their Guru, and made me reflect on the amount of discipline these gurukul kids are into. What kind of education do we, as kshatriyas, get and brahmins here, adopt? We learn all the skills related to mastering various weapons. But brahmins are deeply involved in learning and understanding the multiple mantras. As I am nearing my nine-month delivery period, there is no chance of giving birth at the royal court. My kids would be born here. And apart from their kshatriya routine of learning various astra prayogas, Valmiki Maharshi would also teach them brahmana shlokas. Therefore, they would be raised as both brahmins and kshatriyas. Kshatriya blood is already flowing in their body, so learning the astras would be easy task for them. They might not take much time to learn the art of weaponry compared to the slokas and mantras. I doubt if they can even pronounce all the words perfectly. I should take extra care, even though Valmiki Maharshi will guide them in chanting rightly. I should also make them practice enough before their every session.

I should also take extra care in making my kids build good relationships with their friends. They should be able to mingle well and not act in a discriminatory way as they are kshatriyas. I know I cannot hide their varna for long, but I should try inculcating unbiased values.

And beyond all of this, there is one primary and essential thing that I should be very careful about. I cannot completely avoid talking about this subject, but one that I should be very vigilant about. They should not know at any instance, up to some level, that they are Rama's children and I am Sita. If they know about their lineage, they would pester me with several questions as to why are they here somewhere in the ashram, far from Ayodhya. Children love to spend their time with their fathers and here, rather than being with their kingly father, who would like to stay in this ashram, leaving the glorious Ayodhya. They would not and even force me to go with them to Ayodhya. They are too young to understand the complexities surrounding the issue of chastity, and my birth would be a disaster if they encountered such words from some common public. I want their minds to be free and clean, not corrupted by all these unnecessary and unwanted thoughts. They should be equivalent to their father in the heart, soul, and noble work they perform.

I do not know how they are to encounter their father and how they will. Still, as far as I and this hermitage are concerned, we would ensure to place them in anonymity, and I will bring them up in such a way that when they encounter each other, Rama would understand that they are his children. This is my sole purpose.

When I thought about leaving the world and going, my kids inside me became my strength, and they provided me with the courage to live. When I thought I could not live, not even a day without my Rama beside me, I succeeded in living these many days. Our blood inside me has been my motivation to survive. I have dedicated my complete self as a wife to Rama and as a queen to Ayodhya. Now I should also give my entire self as a successful mother. My children should rule the nations with equal and more grace and dignity compared to their father. They should set their own identity and should win hearts with their efficient ruling where the poor and the needy should be able to live their lives in satisfaction. There should be no needy begging for alms. People should be happy with their rule. No cry of hunger and no cry of pain. Whether protecting their people from external enemies or self-protecting their nation from natural disasters; my children should be uncompromised. These thoughts are giving me enough strength every day. I have a strong future in my womb.

While thinking I feel they are listening to my thoughts and are giving their nod by kicking my stomach. I am relieved with these kicks. I started talking to them. "Do you also want to be good rulers?" Before speaking further, I waited eagerly for their kick. "Seems you are sleeping. Maybe I will talk with you after some time." As I was about to stop talking, I heard their kick and considered it a yes. But asking these complex questions is beyond their age.

***

I have stepped into the ninth month of my pregnancy; the womb appears complete. Now only a few days to see my dear Rama's form on earth. In a few days, I am going to be a mother. A few days for Rama to be a father and a few days for the Ikshvaku kingdom to get its descendants. My mothers-in-law Kausalya, Sumitra and Kaikeyi will be grandmothers and Lakshmana, Bharata and Shatrugna will soon be uncles. While I was connecting all the relations, only my dear father-in-law King Dasharath, came to my mind. Had King Dasharath been alive, he would be the happiest person to see his grandchildren. He had waited so much for children and did so many yagnas with his wives, and holding grandchildren in his arms would make him really happy. But I firmly believe that he shall be watching us and continues to bless us and the kingdom.

Meanwhile, the festive ambience is in the air. While everybody is happy, waiting for the auspicious day, I had just one thought in my mind. Would my dear Rama be thinking about his children? After these many months of being away, will he still remember me? Will he be waiting for his children? Or, because the dynasty needs its descendants, will he be forced to marry someone? I know my Rama, he is Ekapatnivrathudu, and I can never even imagine him thinking about another woman. While I trust him to this extent, the only thought that should actually be sidelined is disturbing me. What if Rama is forced to marry by some external people for the sake of mere descendants? My Rama, who promised to put public interest before him, will he marry for people's interest? This is the question that is pricking me like a thorn.

Every time when everything is happy, there will constantly be one thought that makes me unhappy. I feel like going back to Ayodhya to check the kingdom's status. Parallelly, when Rama was alone, and while I was at Ravana Lanka, did Rama ever get thoughts like these? Will Sita bow to the demands of the Dashagriva Ravana? But Rama never questioned me after coming back from Lanka. I did the fire ordeal to prove my purity to the public and not my husband. These thoughts helped me suppress my suspicion against my dear Rama.

I am Sita, and I am the great Rama's wife. It's a disgraceful thing to let my mind allow such ill thoughts. With Rama's blood blooming inside me, it is a shame on my part to think about all of these, drawing a line to my own past. It seems something is not well with me. I usually put behind all the negative thoughts the second I receive them. When I was abducted by Ravana forcefully, even now, when I think of this incident, it leaves me dumbstruck. Only I know the pain that I have gone through. I thought to help the sadhu. But that was Ravana in disguise. He lifted me along with the land and took me to his kingdom. I was abducted by some unknown man, held as a captive, yet offered to become his queen. I bore mental torture every day with so many lankinis around me. I was unknown of the present and future. Secondly, I was worried about my Rama and the harsh words I spoke to Lakshmana, because of which he left me alone and went in search of Rama. Perplexed with various thoughts if they would ever come to the rescue or will they even know what happened, if they come, will war occur? It's not even about war; it's about the after-effects of war that worry a woman. This is me and the pessimistic outlook I developed during my days of captivity. Though I have overcome it with my strong attitude, the effect of the stay in Lanka is still prevalent.

***

I generally think about an issue, decide on its outcome and leave the matter then and there. But my psyche has changed these days. Living in the present, I think about the past and calculate my future. Now that I am not just Rama's wife and Ayodhya's queen but going to be a mother, I should stop overthinking. If not, the effect is going to be on my kids. I should be an excellent mother to them. I know they will make their parents proud and spread their name and fame across Ayodhya. But the difficult task, as I always ponder, is being a single mother to my kids. It's not easy to bring them up. Mother and father play their roles in bringing up kids. A mother teaches the kid how to be patient enough and helps develop the spirit of kindness and compassion. In my opinion, mothers play a vital role in instilling good values that make up a character.

A kshatriya father trains the children's minds and makes them aware of the pros and cons of the distant kingdoms. How to be formidable in battle, how to rule a kingdom efficiently, how to treat personal and princely life equally, without affecting each other, how to answer enemy threats, how to look after public demands, how to select the kingdom's council of ministers, how to wage war, the type of astras to put into use and how to safeguard the kingdom during natural calamities, as these are quite unimaginable and uncontrollable. Any king can rule the kingdom while the empire is blooming without any problems. Still, only an efficient leader can put the empire on track from the various problems and resume operations. While ruling and protection go, on one hand, making the kingdom prosper goes on the other.

A king should not only look at solving the problems but should ensure that the kingdom blooms and the name and fame of the kingdom travel beyond space and time. A king would train their princes in this manner. But as my kids will not be with Rama, Valmiki Maharshi can train them on one level, in the astra prayogam, reading the Vedic texts, and learning the chants. I am forever indebted to him for the help.

But now, this is not the right time to evaluate how a mother and father can coincide in bringing up their children. I should take the responsibility to never make them feel the absence of their father. My father has brought me up not just like a damsel but also raised me by educating me about the workings of an empire. There are instances when courtiers around would laugh at a king's interest in a princess, as her role is to get married to a prince, be a mother and rear a child.

I used to ask my father, "Father, you are bringing me up like a prince; you are teaching me all the needed essentials for a prince. Will they ever help me in the future? Soon I will be married off to a prince, and I will stay in the kingdom. Will these lessons help me at all?"

My father replied, "Sita, since the moment I saw you while ploughing for the yagna, till now, I never felt you are my daughter and the Mithila's little princess. I always brought you up like my son and Mithila's prince. Even though you will be married soon and shall go to your in-laws' place, these skills will help you one day and you will know my motive. If you have observed some Mithilians, you find them going to nearby wells to learn the act of swimming. Floods to Mithila would be a nearly impossible act, but still, they learn to swim. Why? Because it is a life skill. This skill might not help only themselves, but in life, they might encounter a situation where this act of swimming would help to save other's life. I hope now you understand the reason behind teaching and preaching all these skills. There is nothing wrong in learning a new thing."

These words are circulating in my mind now. The time that my dear father mentioned has come now. I am thankful to my father, who did the unusual activity of raising a daughter like a son. Now, even in the absence of their father, I will take the dual task of raising the kids. They would learn both compassion and mental agility. I would pass on the stories of various rulers that my father taught me and the stories that I learned from my own experiences and Rama, during my short stay at Ayodhya. I would equip and make them ready so that when the day comes, the day when I hand over the kids to their beloved father, they would be prepared to take charge. My Rama should overflow in happiness to see his own form in his children. While daydreaming, I think it's better to use the word future-reading myself; I heard Valmiki Maharshi calling my name. He would have called me several times, but because I was so deeply immersed in my own world, I couldn't pay attention. He would have just finished teaching mantras to kids and, seeing me in a reflective state, would have called me.

"Sita Mata! It seems you are not in this world. Your focus is somewhere else. I have called you a couple of times. What happened? Is everything alright? If you are in such a deep thought, it would definitely be about Janakirama. I understand how it is to raise children without the father's moral support."

"Yes, Maharshi, you are right. I am thinking about how to bring children up in their father's absence. I am not worried but excited to bring them up, just how their father would have brought them up if he is with them", I said with a strong voice.

"Sita Mata! Have you thought about naming your kids?"

"Swami, I am not as well-equipped in various shastras as you are. Is there anything in this entire world that you are not aware of? It's not right on your part to come and ask me about their names. You are like their grandfather; you should name them", I said with a tone of request.

"I will think of the names. I should also sit and study the time they are born and shall name them accordingly. A person's success and future depend on the name. I will name your kids in such a manner that their rule is not only limited to Ayodhya but the entire country, their name should travel and should be heard in every nook and corner of the city. Their rule should be as powerful and efficient as their father's. And I will also have to fix an auspicious muhurta for their naming ceremony. I will also have to invite several rishis and saints from other hermitages to witness this auspicious ceremony. Please be seated, Mata. It's not advisable to stand for long hours. I will take your leave and proceed to look after the arrangements", Valmiki left.

These days I am not able to stand for long hours. The weight on my womb is not letting me stand. I am dehydrating quickly, and not able to concentrate on work continuously. I am not even experiencing food cravings. It's causing a lot of physical pain. But as every mother can relate, we do not get carried away by the pain, and the most awaited moment makes us forget all the pains. Nine months, nine long months, the kids breathe with us, sleep with us, listen to us, and occasionally reply to our questions with their kicks. How they slowly develop their body organs from a little embryo is fascinating.

***

All of a sudden, I can feel something strange. My head feels like someone has held it tight with their hands, not with a rope. I could feel every strand of my long thick hair. Someone is pulling it hard. My vision started getting blurred. Everything that appeared stable has now begun to appear in double. I am also not smelling pleasant; I am attached to some unpleasant smell that I have never experienced before. I have also started biting my teeth, and my lips are becoming dry. My hands became numb, and I was unable to move my fingers. My legs started shivering, and my feet turned cold. And with immense pressure on my stomach, I started screaming at once. I shouted at the top of my voice. People around me were startled to see me shout with such pain. They have held me tight. And I could vaguely see people from far running towards me.

I was soon laid down on some horizontal bed-like thing made out of the grass. I could sense the roughness of the leaves. They are actually pricking my back slightly. I was taken to my hut and soon surrounded by the eldest women in the hermitage.

They were all discussing something very serious, and so much hullabaloo was going around. They were asking for some cloth. Everything is dark. I can see nothing. I can sense nothing.

I hear not a single sound. I could only hear two babies crying at the end of their voices. It's definitely not at a very long distance. It's somewhere very near, and it's near my ears. I could also feel the tender skin layered with some sticky substance. It smells like blood. At once, I hugged them very tightly, touching their head, delicate hands, and legs softly. I pecked a very tight kiss on their forehead and on their little eyes which are yet to open, their soft hands, and tiny little feet. They are our two sons and little twins. I wish Rama would have been here to see them.

Their eyes and sharp nose look precisely like Rama's. One old woman has come forward to put them in a little swing made out of many forest leaves and branches. It looks so attractive and is decorated with colourful flowers. This is why the room is also filled with the scent of these flowers. It's not one particular scent but a multitude of fragrances. Some are emitting a powerful smell, which is also a bit suffocating. But the decoration is mesmerizing enough to suppress the smell of the scents. As I am experiencing all these, the old woman is still standing beside me to take the kids, clean the outer layer, and put them in the swing.

By whispering Rama-nama into their ears and kissing on their forehead, I didn't want to give them, but still, with so much difficulty, I handed them over to the old lady. She took both of them in a soft cotton cloth and started cleaning all the thick layered skin topped with blood. She then placed them in a single long leaf and took them to the outer room. I could hear some men's voices. Perhaps, it should be Valmiki Maharshi. She would have taken kids to seek his blessings.

The babies are still crying out very loud, so loud that the entire hermitage can come to know about the birth of two babies. It seems as if their voice is going beyond the abbey. Not just beyond it, but it feels as if with the kids' loud cries, even Lord Rama can hear and come to know about their birth. But just for a moment, it was complete silence. I guess Valmiki Maharshi is blessing them. Now I am experiencing the best feeling any woman in the world could get. Motherhood. It is such a blessing. To be able to give birth to new lives and see them for the very first time, joy is beyond any set boundary.

Now I understand how valuable life is. When Rama initially deserted me, I thought of taking my life. I was on the verge of giving up. I tried to keep my spirits up, but the thought that Rama, my dear Rama had deserted me blew my mind away. I could not believe it for a moment. I thought my travel to the hermitages was temporary, to take the blessings for my unborn babies. Hearing that I am to be here permanently made me sick. I was questioning my existence. Is it for this I demanded Rama take me along to the perilous forest, even though he denied it?

Is it for this that I battled my mind and the grievous and dreadful Ravana? Is it for this that I performed a fire ordeal that no woman could have done? I was so very pensive and adamant about taking my life. If Lakshmana would not ask me to swear and if I was not carrying babies in my womb, I would not have waited for a second. Ikshvaku lineage would have come to an end with me. But now, I regret my suicidal thoughts.

Maybe this is why elders say we should never decide when we are angry or sorrowful. If I had decided then, it would not just ruin my name but also the entire Ikshvaku dynasty. Time is the only thing that answers every question in life. My two sons did a job beyond their life, saving me even before birth. Now, after facing separation from my dear Rama for these many months, I understand the need to self-motivate myself constantly, and the result is the endless joy that I see right in front of me. From now on, I should be vigilant enough to raise my kids to the best of my capacity and possibility.

The old lady has brought twin sons inside and put them in the swing. Their cry seems to have subsided now, and they have not opened their eyes yet. Every mother understands how it feels to first see their son's eyes. I am keenly observing their eyes, the movement of eyeballs inside them, so that I do not miss the sight when they open their eyes for the very first time. My eyes are fixed on their face now. I blurred the entire surroundings and muted my ears.

I was about to yawn and saw the babies' eyelids, and much to my surprise, the eyes opened, stopping my yawn halfway. I have seen the world's most precious jewels in front of me. I stood up with great difficulty, strolled towards them, and kissed their eyes. But as soon as they opened their eyes, it seemed as if they were staring at something so intensely. They have stopped crying and are now staring continuously without even blinking their eyes. Even if I cannot guess what they are into; no one can understand the thought process of the kids as soon as they are born.

I was advised to take a rest for a few days. While spending this part of my life in bed most of the time, the kids are with me. They are either having milk or sleeping. Much to my surprise, they are fond of playing with each other. Their sleep timings are also completely unusual; because of them, my sleep pattern has also been modified. Now I do not have a fixed sleep pattern, because of which I have completely lost track of time.

What part is day and what part of it is night, I do not know. As I am restricted from doing some daily chores, most of my time is spent whiling away with my thoughts. This time, I am not thinking about my past or future but the present situation of my two kids. They even giggle at the most unusual times when it's completely dark and silent. They are so loud that sometimes, they even disturb the sleep of some of the hermitage people.

We are currently spending most time together, the only stage in life where we three spend time together. Because by the time they start crawling, none can stop them. They initially crawl and walk limply; once they start walking, they would fly like baby birds. Suddenly I was reminded of the three eggs and their mother. The last morning, I saw the nest, but I did not find their mother bird. I hope their mother has come.

***

Valmiki Maharshi is busy meeting many people for the auspicious naming ceremony. He is very much particular about it. Two days before the naming ceremony, the hullabaloo has begun. It felt like it was the first ceremony that people are celebrating for a long time. I can see a tremendous amount of joy, and beyond age, kids, old people, everybody is contributing. I feel sick and tired from just watching them work. I want to go and tell them to stop working. I want the naming ceremony to come in a wink so that the hermitage people will at least have some rest.

As I always wished, the auspicious day has finally come. The ashram usually looks ordinary, and the flowers are scattered here and there. The entire place is very organized, and the swing is decorated beautifully. This swing seems to be even more majestic than the previous one. It is artistically decorated with flowers of different colours and beautifully woven leaves. Even more beautiful are the eye-catching dresses of the twin brothers.

They both wore half dhotis in two different colours. One in bright yellow, and the other wore dark blue. Besides their dhotis, something that struck my attention was the ornaments that kids wore around their necks, hands, and head. It is a bright white-coloured long chain beaded with pearls. These ornaments are identical, and the beads are so much in the same shape and size that they must have been woven by an experienced handmade jewellery maker.

Everyone got alerted upon the arrival of Valmiki Maharshi at the venue. He indicated the start of chanting of the mantras by the pandits. Amid the chanting of these mantras; amid the religious pandits, amid the cheers of the old and young men and women, Valmiki arrived. Everybody and I are so excited to know these twins' names. Now onwards, I will call them by completely different names that I have never called before. Every day since their birth, I called them by the names of my choice, which come to my mind at that point.

But now they will have a name. The world will know them by their special name. I am unable to hold back my anxiety. Valmiki Maharshi went to the two kids. He first took the elder one and whispered his name. He then took the younger one and whispered his name. It would be unclear, as it was just whispering.

He then called, "Sita Mata, please come here."

Maharshi whispered the elder son's name in my ear and asked me to repeat the same three times. By thinking about Rama in my heart, I have whispered his name. I repeated the same for the younger son.

Good names, I thought. Still, the people are looking forward to knowing their names.

Valmiki Maharshi lifted the elder one above his head as high as possible and announced his name as Kusha. People clapped and repeated the name amidst themselves as Kusha. Kusha. Kusha. And Maharshi then proceeded by lifting my younger son, aloof, and announced his name as Lava. People with continuous clapping repeated the name again and again. Interestingly, they started to call them together Lava Kusha, Lava Kusha, Lava Kusha.

Lava and Kusha are such lovely names. But what could be the meaning behind these names? I started to test my knowledge to the best possible extent. But I am unable to guess the exact meaning. After reaching my maximum thinking capability, I gave up. I quickly hurried to Maharshi even before he could start a new action plan with the kids. "Maharshi, the two names Lava and Kusha, is soothing to the ears. But as you won't name them without any meaningful significance. I would like to know the meaning behind these names."

"Yes, Sita Mata, I decided upon their names after much research. The elder one is named Kusha since he was rubbed and cleaned with the Kusha grass. While Lava is dried with the roots of the grass, he is named Lava. I have taken their names from the materials they were cleaned and dried."

I wondered, knowing the significance. Taking the blessings of Valmiki Maharshi, I now took his leave.

***

The kids are too young to narrate the brave stories of Lord Rama. But still, I heard from a lot of people saying that young kids will have a lot of concentration and hence whatever we input shall stay in their subconscious minds. Therefore, I started narrating the words of Rama regarding satyam, dharmam, shantam so on. Amongst these two, Lava appears to be the naughtiest. While Kusha is staring at me continuously and is listening with so much concentration, without even winking his eyes, Lava is not even trying to make eye contact. He is looking somewhere else and is simply enjoying his own company.

Nothing seems to entertain him as much as his own company. Sometimes, he claps; sometimes, he kicks Kusha; sometimes turns his little body in a complete posture as if he is hugging him. And sometimes he cries out very loud that seeing him, even Kusha starts crying. The funniest part is that when I narrate a very serious story, Lava starts bursting out in laughter; he even holds my little finger and swings his body, making me dance with him. Meanwhile, Kusha is entirely a silent kid, listening to my narration with his eyes wide open.

The hardest part is to make them sleep at night. The irregular sleep schedule that has begun during their delivery is continuing. They are in deep sleep most mornings and never sleep at night. While it is a near herculean task to make one kid sleep, making two kids sleep is even more difficult. But, after some days, I found two tricks for putting them to sleep. One is swinging them at a medium pace without stopping for long. Lava, the naughtiest, would be the first to sleep in this manner. Secondly, I would make them sleep on their back and beat them gently till I found them asleep. Putting them to sleep makes me feel like I have won a war. With the discovery of these two tricks, I have now found the way to my regular sleep cycle.

***

"Mother, how is my new dhoti for the first day of my gurukul?" asked Lava.

"Lava, you look so charming and excited", I said.

"Yes, mother, till now, we have learnt so many lessons by sleeping on your lap. You taught us many stories from the life of Lord Rama, and many mantras, which we even chant every day. But today is the first day of the change of teacher. From our mother as our first teacher to Maharshi Valmiki as our next teacher, we are very excited to learn many things like archery, warfare, and the chanting of slokas. Mother, you taught us how to be good humans. Today we are putting our first step in learning how to protect ourselves. We are excited to learn as these will also help us protect you. Please bless me, mother." Lava touched my feet and took blessings. Before leaving, he came and hugged me.

I was amazed and shocked to see Lava at such a level of maturity. From thinking about protecting himself to thinking about me. Is this the same Lava who was the naughtiest? Is this the same Lava who never paid attention while narrating the stories and looks everywhere except at my eyes? I could not believe seeing him grow so much mentally. To reveal my innermost feeling to you, I am very proud of my Lava. He is still waiting near the door. "Lava, it's time for you to go. Why are you still waiting? And…"

Kusha interrupted my speech, and seeing his younger brother waiting, he took my blessings. I have held his shoulders and took dristi and waved them bye. Staring at the two kids, going to the ashram hand in hand, I thought they should always be together in life no matter the consequence or problem they face.

Lava and Kusha are attending their first Vedic classes with several other students. They are seated around a large and tall peepal tree in the ashram's very centre. With several students chanting the mantras, the entire place is vibrating. The first session went for three hours. It is their first long class. Kusha appears to be a little tired, but Lava still has the same energy that he began the session. Today was just the chanting class, and in between, Maharshi was asking some questions.

Lava came running to me. Seeing him, Kusha also started to run. By taking blessings, he just came and started narrating how his first day was and what he learnt. Even though I had observed everything, I paid attention to Lava's speech keenly, as if I were a first-time listener. Then Kusha started complaining about Lava pestering Valmiki Maharshi too much by asking many questions. Agreeing with his mistake, Lava expressed that those were his real concerns. "Mother,

If I get any doubts, I would clarify them then and there, only then I can concentrate on the next topic, and most importantly, I get a peaceful sleep. But mother, hereafter, I won't pester Maharshi with too many questions. I will root away all the unimportant ones." Yes, Lava asks too many questions while the other explains something. Even while I was describing or narrating some stories, he used to ask many doubts. After feeding them their favourite dishes, I put them both to sleep.

The next morning, when Lava and Kusha were about to leave for school, and while taking blessings, I told Lava, "Lava, what did I tell you yesterday."

"Mother, do not think I forget easily. As promised, I will not trouble Maharshi and the other students by asking too many questions."

"That's my boy." I wished them all the very best for today's practical class for learning archery and martial skills. But today, I cannot see how they are performing because Valmiki Maharshi took them to the nearby forest. So, I eagerly waited for their return.

This time, Lava did not come running; instead, Kusha came and said they learnt archery. Lava, by pressing his right hand against his shoulder, "Mother, when you were narrating us the stories about Rama and his efficiency and perfection in archery, I thought it would be an easy task to accomplish. But no, I was wrong. You do not understand, mother, how difficult it is. Today, I could not properly place the arrow in the bow, leave alone hitting the target. But one day, I would sure hit the target like Rama. I would aim the bull's eye." By applying churn made out of medicinal herbs, I gave him the word strength.

Kusha seems alright, as he would not have done so much in abundance on the first day, unlike Lava. Lava learns anything as if he had to learn everything on the first day. But Kusha, born minutes before Lava, is way more mature than Lava. His maturity is seen in every act he does. Even though archery would have thrilled him so much, he would not have tried beyond his limit.

***

These days, I am becoming busier, and having less time for myself, unlike the previous days. I become busy preparing these two kids in the morning, making them ready, and afternoons while away listening to their narration. Each narrates their version of the day. They highlight entirely different things, unlike each other; they complain for some time and then hug each other. Due to the strenuous activity in the morning, both of them slept very early, and my storytelling time started reducing. My sleep cycle is getting back to normal these days.

Alongside archery and martial skills classes, Maharshi Valmiki also teaches them music. Due to their tight schedule, Lava and Kusha seem so engaged that they just come and sleep as soon as they finish their gurukul. Nowadays, they do not have any time to narrate the day-to-day happenings and have even almost stopped quarrelling and complaining about each other. I will forget all the stories if this continues for some days.

One day, as they went to the archery classes, Lava came running to me. I was a bit shocked to see him. Because he usually has a sense of joy or a feeling of tiredness when he comes running. But today, he does not have both of them. He came running as fast as he could. By holding his breath, he at once fell on my feet. "Mother, you asked me to be very careful while shooting with the arrows, as they are very sharp. But today, I made a grave error when we went for the archery practice. I have taken the life of a deer. Guruji asked me to shoot at the bark of a distant tree. I aimed correctly. I was in a proper position, but only when I released the arrow from my hand did, I see a deer coming in between me and the bark, and the arrow hit the deer's neck. I could neither stop the arrow as it was already released nor the deer, which came out of nowhere.

Usually, before the practice session begins, Valmiki Maharshi checks if everything is alright and only then signals us to begin the session. But today, even after the clearance, the deer came in between and was hit. The arrow was so sharp that it went from this side of the neck to that side. The blood was flowing like a brook. The least satisfactory part is that it has come with its baby deer, and she is safe. But still, she lost her mother and was looking for help wandering here and there. She stood in front of her mother's body most of the time and did not move. Then while we were leaving, we saw her sleeping under a tree. Mother, today, my act of mistake has separated a baby from her mother. She and her mother would have gone on many early morning walks, and her mother would have guided her on many aspects, like how to escape from cruel creatures that await to hunt the deer. I feel despondent for the mother and the baby as well. I am sorry mother, please forgive me. Please forgive your little son. I will be even more cautious."

Lava started crying so much that he was not stopping, even though I tried many ways. I wiped his tears and made him sit pleasantly. "My dear Lava, I completely understand your pain. You did it unintentionally. And secondly, as a beginner, Valmiki Maharshi usually says you should be more cautious. You should not just use your sense of sight to check if there is any animal that is coming because eyes deceive us sometimes. You should also use your ears. But it is not your mistake; you are still in the learning process. Only experienced archers know it. Before practising in the wild, they look and use their ears and check if there is any slight sound that they can hear near them and the impulse closely goes to their fingers, which halts their activity."

"Yes, mother, you are right. But how are you so well-versed in this kind of archery-related thing? You said it so correctly. And your answer is the same as Maharshi Valmiki's answer. That's why now I understand why Maharshi is giving us sound practice every day. Thank you, mother, for providing me with moral support."

Only I know how I am aware of all of these stories. Rama, as he used to go hunting while we spent our time at the Vanavas, used to narrate stories about how he saved some animals. I cannot answer Lava's question about how I know all these tactics. It's because of his own father, which I cannot disclose to them now. They are chanting his name every day, revering my dear Rama as the King of Ayodhya and as their God. If I tell them that the person whom they thought they would never meet in their life is their own father, there would be no sons in the world as happy as them. And if Rama knows that he has twin sons, he would be the happiest father in the world. I know they both will meet at one point in their life, I will make my sons great as my dear Rama, and then I will hand them over to him and happily go to my mother's lap as already promised.

***

With days passing so quickly, one day, Lava and Kusha started to sing. I thought it was like an everyday practice but something different. Usually, I would be the only audience, but today there is so much crowd that they are not visible. People surrounded so much that they started to sing as a chorus. But what are they singing? I was not able to get the words. I went near to listen to their singing. The nearer I went, the more goosebumps I got. I cannot believe it, and it's beyond my thoughts. They are singing Ramayana. Valmiki has mentioned that he has written Ramayana, but I never expected that Lava and Kusha would sing the verses with such perfection. They are singing so well, adding beauty to Valmiki's verses. When they are singing, I am visualizing every word.

That is Valmiki's greatness and the singing training that the kids received. Usually, Lava would not keep anything a secret, but in this singing episode, they would have known and been practising for days. Still, Lava became successful in keeping it a secret. Today, I received the best morning surprise ever. Any mother feels that their kids are growing very fast, and the same with me. They appear to be growing like a wild bamboo tree overnight. I am not able to focus on both senses of sight and hearing at the same. Seeing them together makes me so proud, and listening to my Rama's story from their mouth is so sweet that it appears they are pouring an elixir into my ears.

As they are singing the greatness of Rama, I can feel Rama's presence beside me, talking. It appears that Rama has come from Ayodhya and is grooving to his sons' tribute. While they are singing, how can I, who know everything about my dear Rama, more than anyone, be away from the Ramayana recitation? Even I started singing praises for Lord Rama. My sons Lava and Kusha are looking at me with amusement about how I know Sri Ramacharitam this deeply. And then the entire ashram air is filled with Rama's story and reverberating with Rama-Nama chanting. Today, they have just limited to one episode of Ramayana. And then Valmiki called Lava and

Kusha and made them sit in their regular teaching place.

"Lava Kusha, when you are chanting Rama-nama, it is like parrots making sweet and pleasant sounds, and it is even more fascinating."

"It is what you have only taught us, Guruvarya," said Lava.

"Do you know why I have taught you the Ramayana, which I have written by putting my heart and soul"?

"Yes, Guruvarya, we get so much virtue if we sing or listen to Ramayana", said Kusha.

"Not just that Kusha, Ramayana, helps build right citizens of a country. It corrects humans' behaviour and forbids us from becoming animals again."

For this, Lava gave an expected reply. "Guruvarya, if you say these many big big things, how do we understand?"

Valmiki, smiling, said, "That's true, my son. These all are immense and divine things. Let's take the characters in the Ramayana. Dasharatha Maharaja never crosses his word. To uphold the word given to her wife, Kaikeyi, he sent his son, Sri Rama Chandra, to the forest and sacrificed his own life. So, what can we infer?"

The ever-exciting Kusha says, "Even if we are to lose our life, we should never break our words or promises like Sri Rama, Ekpatnivratha, protector of dharma, satyavan, for their parents' happiness. He has left his comforts and went to aranyavasam."

Lava added to Maharshi, saying, "Rama has punished the evil and protected the good."

"Yes" added Maharshi. Then Valmiki asked, "What about Sita Devi?"

I was a bit tense when he started saying about his mother, unaware that I am Sita.

Kusha replied, "Sita is a very chaste woman. When her husband went to forests, she followed him and faced many troubles."

Maharshi added, "Not just that, even when Ravana wooed her with so many jewels, she has rejected, forgoing sleep and food, she has always meditated about Rama."

Lava added, "As a result of that penance, she has conjoined with Rama and is happy."

While they are talking about me, I am missing my dear Rama.

Valmiki said, "Chanting Rama's name always gives enough happiness. Lakshmana, Bharata, and Shatrugna, never crossed their brother Rama's words."

Kusha, with so much disgrace, asked, "What about Ravanasura?"

"Don't you know? For wanting another man's wife, destruction has been bestowed upon him, along with his friends and family. My dear sons, the characters in this Ramayana aid in developing a citizen. Until Ramayana is respected, the humans in this world will reach greater heights by following all the morals. As my dear students, both of you should spread this Ramayana epic in various states and countries", said Valmiki.

Kusha replied, "Why not Guruji!"

I am extremely overwhelmed by this task undertaken by Maharshi Valmiki. My Rama's story, unknown that Rama is their father, the two kids are going to spread. Is there any worthy task beyond this? This delights me a lot.

They both stood up with their musical instrument in their hands, and by taking the blessings from Valmiki Maharshi, they began the most celestial and divine task.

Both of them started singing Rama's story melodiously. I was a bit wondering where they will begin telling Rama's story. They started from Dasharatha Maha Raju.

I was amazed at how these young minds understood Rama so profoundly. My two eyes stand insufficient seeing them sing praises for their father and mother. I can imagine and visualize every aspect of their singing. And when they started singing beautiful verses about my swayamvar, I relived those moments. I began to go with the flow of their singing. There is no more beautiful day than Rama coming for my swayamvar. I got ready as I had been doing for months. Even though I heard a lot about him, I thought he would do no different from every other prince from far-off nations who come with so much pomp and grandeur, with so many attendants, and leave unable to string the Shivadhanassu. But Rama's arrival was so peaceful as a calm river. He did not come with any grandeur. Nor was there so much fuss about his arrival. Later, I heard someone discussing that Rama was brought to win the hand of my marriage without even letting him know about it. Because only a guru can estimate the greatness of his shishya. Vishvamitra has rightly felt that only I am Rama's suitable wife.

When they sang the most beautiful and joyous moment in my life, I became very emotional. After getting married to Rama, how many days did I spend in Ayodhya? How many days was I able to serve my in-laws? With the halting of the crowning ceremony, Rama obliged his father's wish, and we spent our time in the forest.

I followed him, and there we faced several difficulties. Every day in the forest is an arduous task. And from there, when I thought everything was alright, Ravana abducted me, and there the inexpressible agony found my way. After the destruction of Ravana, when I thought Rama would accept me, he just said one word, which still hurts me, "I have saved you. It's my duty. Now you can go where ever you want." But I decided to test my chastity, and I followed Rama. Later on, when everything went well with the coronation, I was sent to the forest. I could not control my tears. I have never lived the life of an ordinary wife. By the time I have journeyed so many years of my life. They have finished singing for this session.

Valmiki is seen advising Lava and Kusha as to how they should sing. He is primarily telling them to sing so that Ramayana will remain forever close in people's hearts. They took the leave of Maharshi.

Lava and Kusha, as usual, are found imitating bird noise. Before times, when they imitated the same, I would act in accordance with what they wished. If they make the hissing sound of a snake, I will act as if I am scared of that snake. And would climb the cot to escape the snake, intensify their emotion and make them happy. I would even scream slightly. Lava and Kusha enjoy this activity so much. They do this most of the time while they are back from Valmiki. But, today, even though they are making a bird sound, I cannot react to anything. They tried "Koo, Koo." But still, I have not responded. Out of disappointment, they came running to me.

Extremely worried, Kusha asked, "Mother, did we make any mistake?"

"Did we hurt you, mother?" asked Lava.

And both started asking, "Then why are your eyes filled with tears, Mother? We are your brave kids. If you ask, we can even get the golden mountain, Mother. But what is why your eyes are filled with tears, Mother? If we cannot reduce your sorrow, what is the purpose of a son's life."

Hugging Lava and Kusha tightly in my arms and wiping my tears, "No, my dear sons, nothing. Why will I feel sad when you are there to wipe my tears? These are just happy tears from listening to your Ramayana."

Cutting my speech out, by just listening that I am happy because of their singing, Kusha spoke, "Mother, if you are this content, how happy will Sita Rama be if they listen to our singing Mother? Please take us to Ayodhya", requested Kusha.

"If we sing Ramayana in front of Lord Rama, in Rama's place, how happy will Rama be? Seeing him happy, we will also be happy, mother", opined Lava.

"I am doing so much penance to make that happen. If Guru wishes you to send, you can go", I spoke.

Again, cutting my speech short, Lava exclaimed, "Then mother, we will at once go and ask Guru himself."

"See, my dear kids, he will only send you when the time comes," I spoke.

"We will obey your words, Mother. Today, Valmiki Maharshi will teach us how to leave divyastras, we will take your leave, bless us, mother", and they ran.

***

By evening Lava and Kusha came running to my place and explained all about the usage of the divyastras. "Mother, though we got these astras, we were asked to use them only during huge war. And, mother, we have another happy news for you. Your penance has got its result. Valmiki Maharshi has permitted us to go sing Ramayana at Ayodhya."

Tears started rolling down my eyes after hearing such amazing news that both sons and father would see each other for the first time. Lava, "Mother, why have you started to cry again? Don't you like us to go to Ayodhya?"

"No, my dear sons, the thought that you are going as street singers to Ayodhya is making me reflect upon so many things," I said.

Kusha replied, "We are not scared, Mother. You are a brave mother. Are we not your sons? We can sing Ramayana."

"We can also fight." Lava said in anger. "That is what scares me, my sons."

"No, mother, never. We don't. Please bless us and send mother. We would see Sree Rama with our naked eyes. Until now, we only heard about him and sang praises for Rama. But we never saw." Lava Kusha said.

"Please, see my dear sons. Have my eyes also and see. See him and be happy", I said.

"Sure, mother," they said.

"I forgot to tell you. Do not accept any gifts from anyone."

"Why do we need gifts and presents, mother? Able to see Sree Rama itself is the biggest gift."

"Yes, my dear sons." By handing them over their small bag with sufficient dresses for their stay at Ayodhya, and their musical instruments, I waved them bye, by kissing their forehead. They seem to be happy and blissful, going to see their Rama.

Even though I told them not to misbehave at Ayodhya at any cost, I am still afraid of Lava, who cannot tolerate any pain inferred upon him. Kusha thinks before he speaks, whereas Lava does not. Kusha forgives anyone even if they have caused him inconvenience. Lava speaks frankly and does not tolerate any action.

But did I do the right task by sending my sons Lava and Kusha to their father's place? This sense of fear and apprehension is tormenting me. What if my Rama identifies his sons? Will the rishis, who are said to be endowed with the highest cognitive abilities recognize Rama's sons and unite them? Will the reunion between Rama and his sons happen now? Fearing the future, I have asked Valmiki Maharshi to let me be in anonymity. I have been successful in not revealing my name and whereabouts for more than ten years. Lava and Kusha have asked me many times till now. They have asked me about our family.

"Mother, are we only three in our family? We have our friends in the gurukul talking about their fathers, grandmothers, grandfathers, and relatives with whom they play on holidays. But why are we only three? Where is our father? Do we not have any sisters? Do we not have any cousins to play with? Why should only we be together?"

Beyond all these questions, one question that they keep asking about is their father. When they were kids, when they did not develop that much maturity, when they did not develop that sense of consciousness about their life, I have successfully hidden the dominant question. But as time passed, as they grew older and started gaining consciousness, not even a day passed without them asking about their father. It was a new challenge to find an answer every time they asked me. Sometimes, I tell them their father has gone to earn a living for our family. Hence, after making enough money, he would come and take us away from this ashram. But when I said this kind of answer, it was pretty shocking for them.

What is the need for our father to take us away from here mother? He can also stay with us in the hermitage. Mother, we do not want to miss our family like friends and go out of this place. We want our father and friends too. Beyond missing friends, we would miss the pleasant nature here at the hermitage. I heard that life outside the hermitage is very polluted and unbearable. We heard from our friends whose parents travelled to the outer place. They told the people there are very sophisticated and even more comfortable in isolation than in a company. And the kids spend most of their time at home, without playing. How on earth are we even going to cope with life without friends? Mother, when father comes, please ask him to be at the hermitage itself. Let us all be here, together. I do not know what you do, but you must request our father.

These are the kind of questions they ask. But only I know that I have told them a lie, and only I know that their father has not gone to any distant place. They have three grandmothers to take care of, a huge family, three uncles- Lakshmana, Bharata, and Shatrugna, and three aunties. Beyond their relatives, they have Ayodhyians, ready to sacrifice their lives to their dear King Lord Rama. If I tell them, unlike the decision that they have taken now, they will rethink and revamp their decision. They would be delighted to leave this place to be with their father and family. Even though they might get a new guru at Ayodhya, they will miss their favourite Guru, Valmiki. Their question about sophisticated life, one away from nature, does not even count.

It's been half a day; would these kids have reached Ayodhya? Would the people at Ayodhya like their performance? Would they have listened to the performance with concentration or immersed in their worlds? But since their composition is about their favourite King Rama, they would have come in huge numbers just by listening to the story of Rama's childhood.

People who would be so happy, composed, and elated listening to the stories of Lord Rama in his childhood, youth, and swayamvar, do they still carry the question of chastity, or will they rethink their decision? While one part of my mind is thinking about this, the other half is self-warning, Sita! You are here not to think about that, are Ayodhyians still worried about their mother, all of this should not concern you anymore. It has been more than ten years, and still, you cannot get over it. It is just making me immensely sad. But as you thought before, your focus should now be on raising your kids according to the norms of Lord Rama and modalities of Ayodhya Kingdom. And should hand over your two sons to Lord Rama and go to your mother, as you promised. This inner voice has so much resonated with me that I lost track of my routine. Every day, I water the plants early in the morning, but today I have forgotten to water them. They would be dying in this hot sun. I once left the place, though watering them in this hot sun is not advisable. Still, I do not want to affect their natural process. I felt so much of an apology and went to the plants whose leaves are not so rigid and glossy as they usually appear.

Today I have been taught a good lesson: I should never even think about that episode that separated my Rama from me. But I am just praying for only one thing. Rama should not doubt that these two kids share so many features like him.

***

It's the second day since they have gone. They would have street sung the composition, and I am sure they would have gained the people's appreciation. Would their voice have touched Rama's ears? No, Rama would not let them in if their voice had touched his ears unless it touched his heart. I am sure they would not lose confidence and sing with the same tempo they have sung here, whose result has not just impressed people around the hermitage but also allowed people to participate in chorus.

They went from this place only the day before yesterday, and I started missing them. I am missing their everyday conversations bagged with their requests early in the morning and their everyday evening conversations about their daily class, and their regular complaints as well. More than Kusha's complaints, Lava's complaints cross the fort walls.

Every mother, how adventurous be their sons, how much so powerful they are, would think of only two things. One is if they have adequately eaten, and secondly, if they have slept well. Thinking about this, no mother gets proper sleep while her kids are away from her and prays for their wellness and work to finish successfully. There is absolutely no way to send messages. I have not even tamed any bird to act as some information between us. Hence, all I need to do and can do is wait for them to come.

They should be delighted to meet Lord Sree Rama. But they should be a little bit perplexed about not being able to see Sita. Would they even ask about Sita? Yes, they revere Sita and Rama at the same level. Hence, they would have asked for her. But how would Rama even explain the truth to these two little ones, the outsiders to Ayodhya who do not know what has happened? Will he let them know the truth? Or will he make up some other story? But will the kids believe, as they know Sita would never even try to leave Rama?

Suppose Lava and Kusha have been told the bitter truth. They adore for his kingly attributes, for his humanity, his nondiscriminatory rule, the way he treats his mother and step-mothers without any difference and the way he, even though being a king, listens to his parent's words first. From where they have learnt the way to respect their mother. Valmiki has taught value education from Ramayana, primarily from Rama.

After praising Rama so much and loving Rama beyond their extent, if they know that Rama has sent Sita on a permanent exile, would their tender hearts bear the truth, or will they stop singing the praises they have been singing heartfully?

Even though the concept is beyond their understanding, they are very young to understand more significant concepts like chastity, and they would despise Rama for being what he is. For making such a decision. They would even feel so very sorry for their dear queen Sita. For being separated from their beloved Rama.

Will this decision hurt them? If they know Rama is his father who sent his mother into exile, will they ever return to their father? Or, will they leave their father permanently and decide to stay with me? If this happens, all the efforts that I have made so far will go in vain. They will never agree or accept Rama as their father. How will I even try to explain the actual reason, being people? How will I explain Rama's oath that Rama has promised to place people's interests before his own, and his role as a king is more viable to him than his role as a husband?

I am helpless; I am in no situation where I can even know what is happening, nor can I control what can happen there. I cannot dictate Rama's decision. I completely lost track of my sleep with this precarious thought that I have got. I have to bear the suspense of this thought for two more days till Lava Kusha's arrival. I have lost track of my routine as well. Nothing seems to be in line now. My food, my sleep, everything is around Rama's reply to these young kids' questions.

Even if they come here with the pain that Sita has been forbidden, I should try to clear their misunderstanding. Will I be able to convince them, it is a herculean task? Convincing them of the regular dissimilarities is difficult for me, and convincing them to get back the lost love for Rama will be worse than any.

I did not even realize when I slept thinking about this. I need to wait for one more day. Once in Ravana Lanka, I wanted the days to complete very fast. And this is the second time in my life that I wanted the day to end fast. We all know we want good days to go very slowly, for us to enjoy and relish every moment. And we want the worse days to go as fast as they can, unable to bear and carry the pressure. But the opposite happens in life. In my swayamvar time, the day my dear Rama came has passed so swiftly, and I always, till date, wanted and wished to relive the very day. But today, I do not want it to go either as a normal day at an average pace or a bad day at a slow pace, but I want it to go like another good day at a breakneck speed.

And now, just another night to pass, and my sons would be here in front of me. I am so excited to sleep early today, as once I fall asleep, I would be in my dreams so that I wake up with my sons standing right before my eyes. I should fall asleep fast, but I am not able to. I learnt from a grandmother here that if we stare at an object deeply and with concentration, we will fall asleep faster. So, I am trying to apply this trick now. But it's been so many days since I have focused on a particular thing this long. I first failed at it. And started trying again and again.

***

"Mother, mother," Lava and Kusha are calling me. Am I dreaming, as I have been getting many of their dreams since they left, or did they come? They should be coming in the morning today. Did they come?

And getting back to reality, I understood that it was not a dream, and I finally opened my eyes to see Lava and Kusha standing in front of me. I see their face with question marks, worried about something wrong.

"Lava Kusha, what happened? Why do you have some doubt on your face? Please tell me." I asked.

"Mother, what we saw there at Ayodhya is different from what we heard about Ayodhya", said they.

"What is that?"

"Yes, we have seen Ayodhya as well as the head of the kingdom", said Lava.

"Ah! You have seen Sree Rama… Is he alright?" I asked with so much curiosity.

"Oh. What is there? He is very well. He is eating nicely and sleeping nicely", they said.

"But, why do you overflow with joy, mother, when we utter Rama's name?" both asked at once.

As soon as I heard from my sons that Rama was well, I was really overflown with happiness. I still have many questions to ask them about Rama and Ayodhya, my in-laws, and their well-being, but these two disappeared. They went inside without even staying for a while.

"My dear sons, is it not a happy thing to chant Rama's name?" I asked.

"Oh! Why not even we thought the same? That he is the ideal man, ideal son, we thought he is an ideal human, through you, Valmiki Maharshi, and many other people in the Ashram. But we have understood his real nature after visiting him, only after seeing him."

What! What have these kids understood, and what have they misunderstood about their father and their dear Rama?

"Why? Sons, did Rama say anything to you? Or did he humiliate you? What has happened? Please be clear." I asked

"Mother, If Rama had humiliated us, we would not be that worried." With tears rolling down his cheeks, Lava started being very emotional.

What happened? If Rama did not humiliate them or do anything wrong. Why are two sons so angry about Rama and their visit to Ayodhya? Oh, Lord Sree Rama! What I guessed the worst should not happen. I cannot tolerate the pain.

"Please let me know what happened," I asked.

"Mother! Rama has thrown our dear Sita into the forest. That too, Sita Mata was pregnant, it seems. How did even Rama feel about sending her away to the forest, mother? Our Rama, whom we revere a lot, our Rama out of whose honour we have sung all the praises, our Rama, whom we all love a lot, why is he so cruel, mother? What big mistake did Sita Mata make by sending her into the wilderness? Why, mother? Sita Mata has already faced so many troubles in the past, and again, she has been put to the test due to her stay with that demon Ravana. What big mistake did she make, mother, to send her to forests?" they asked me.

"After singing Ramayana and having Rama's darshan at Ayodhya, we were very much elated to meet Sita Mata. We have asked our Rama about her. To which leave about replying mother, Rama did not even stay for a while, he hurriedly went inside, with so much contempt. We understood that there must be some form of mishappening. But guessing Sita to be thrown out from Ayodhya to the unknown forests all alone was beyond our understanding and thinking capacity. We, even then, shouted out loudly at the zenith of our voice. Sita Mata, Mother Sita, please come out. We have come from Valmiki's hermitage to have your darshan. What happened to you? Why are you hiding somewhere inside? Please come out, Sita Mata. We have even cried out bitterly, but there was still no response or movement from inside."

"Unable to bear our distress Kausalya, Rama's mother, told us what had happened. We were at once aback listening to her words. We did not believe it initially, but the seriousness and graveness of the issue made us think about the matter and why will Rama's mother lie. We know that Rama loves his people so much, but we never knew that he loves his people more than he loves his wife. Did not he even think that his wife was carrying his children and how did he even get the thought to abandon such a pious woman?"

Lava and Kusha are raging in anger and fury that my words fall short of consoling them. I am helpless. What I prayed and expected the most that it should not happen has happened. These two are too small to understand the entire concept. Will their hate for Rama continue to be the same? Or will they even pay attention to my words? Please help me make these kids understand what Rama is and forbid them from hating Rama.

"My dear Lava and Kusha, there must be a bigger reason for Rama to abandon Sita. You are too young to understand that." I said.

I never saw Lava arguing that much before. With his eyes full of fury, "What reason, Mother. It's very hurtful to hear that even you are also supporting a person like him."

Kusha added, "We felt so much sorrow by listening to those words. How much more would Sita have been sad, mother? And what if some cruel animal has killed her? The forest is filled with so many animals. What if she has been killed? Because she is all alone."

These questions are making me so sorrowful. But controlling my sorrow in front of them, I spoke,

"Wrong, my dear sons, elders are equal to Gods. You should not question them like that." I spoke.

Lava raging with fury, stood up and screamed, "Enough, enough of listening to everything. We have lost respect for Lord Rama."

Screaming this out very loud, they have thrown their musical instruments as a revolt against Rama's decision.

With so much anger, they shouted that they would neither sing the holy composition of Lord Rama nor chant his name.

"Please shut your mouths. Do not speak anything. You are too young and making huge criticism of Lord Rama. Do not even dare to do that. How dare you speak ill about a person held high even by several gods? You are showing hatred against a person who Valmiki Maharshi reveres. You deny chanting the name, which is said to eliminate all the evil if chanted. Blaming a person like him, my God, my Sree Rama, I am not your mother, and I won't even accept you to be my children", the pain, the suffering, took my voice to the peak.

They both came running toward me and hugged with the last words I spoke. But with the blame and criticism they imposed on Lord Rama, I could not receive them warmly as I usually do. Full of rage, I have thrown them down, even though it's not ideal and advisable to do so, but still, I have pushed them down. With this activity they usually never expected, they came running to me and hugged again.

"Mother, why mother, you are so angry like goddess Durga. We have never seen you being this angry. Please forgive us, mother. Please forgive us," they begged.

But still, with so much pain and hatred, I have gone away from them. And they started singing praises to calm me down. One episode of their singing is enough to cool me down. With their praises, I started singing along with them, hugged and showed them the sign of forgiveness.

But, as they began singing, I could sense differences in their faces. They still have that sense of anger. It might take some time for them to return to their original state. I am satisfied that I have successfully cooled them down and reduced their anger toward their father. Seeing them together gave me so much pride and made me sleep well.

***

The day started well, but as soon as the day began, somewhere deep in my subconscious, I was again not feeling well. This time it's not about whether the kids love Rama or not. Something bigger seems to come my way. Even the weather, which was sunny till now, started to be windy. The birds singing in happiness initially started going to their nests due to the harsh weather conditions. They all are seen protecting their babies from the destruction the weather is causing.

Like the day I was abandoned to the forest, the same sense of mystery surrounds me again. Why is this happening to me? Before the kids were sent to Ayodhya, I wanted them to meet their father. While planning to go to Ayodhya, I was afraid their father, Rama, would identify them. While they were at Ayodhya, I did not even get enough sleep because of the dooming thoughts, if they have eaten, if they have slept well, if people over there have accepted their singing, if they have been allowed to go inside and meet Rama, if they were happy with the musical composition. Again the thought of them asking about

Rama's wife, Sita has pestered me. Later on, after their arrival, my happiness could not even stay for some time. They have started hating Rama, and I took time to convince them and remove their hatred.

Now my heart, mind, and the weather seem to be worried over the arrival of someone. Is Rama going to come in search of these two kids? And with this, will he come and take away my children? Or ask who their mother is? Will he see me?

These are making me sick. I just sat at one place and started to brood over my thoughts, hiding from outside as I thought that someone from Ayodhya might arrive today.

***

As the horse steps are nearing, I am convinced that it's not the four brothers, as I am not listening to any cartage sound. It's just the horses. And wait, now I can listen to some people who have come down from the horses. Seems like an army. As the footsteps started coming near, uncertain who they actually were, I went inside.

I saw a group of soldiers from Ayodhya, and I could identify their dress code. Even though it has been many years, I still remember their dress code. The last I saw them was while coming out with Lakshmana, knowing it was a temporary stay.

But why did they even come? Did they come just with some news from Ayodhya as they usually do, or did they come to ask something from Valmiki Maharshi? Because it's just been a day since my children arrived home after their visit from Ayodhya. I am not clear. But let me listen secretly.

Valmiki Maharshi has just gone outside to greet them. Yes, as I have guessed, they are from Ayodhya.

"What's the matter? What made you come here from Ayodhya?" asked Valmiki.

"Swami, you know everything. There is nothing in the world that you are unaware of. Our king Sree Rama is conducting a yagna by name Ashvamedha Yagna, for the world's prosperity. Hence, he has invited you to come along with your students for the yagna."

"Such a pleasant news. Why won't we come if our dear Lord is performing a yagna. By the time yagna comes to an end, we will definitely come", said Valmiki.

They did not notice me, nor did they ask any question, and so it's for inviting Valmiki Maharshi, they have come. But suddenly, I was doomed to one question. No king in this world performs a yagna without their wife, as per my knowledge. But how is it possible for Rama to perform such a yagna? To clarify, I went to a sage nearby and asked him, "Swami, can a king perform yagna without his wife." Instantly he replied, "No, mother. It's not possible."

My heart skipped a beat at once. I, somewhere deep down in my heart, wished to negate my question and say that yes, a king can do yagna without his wife.

But he outrightly replied no. In a way, I felt very harsh to even think of.

Even though I knew a king couldn't perform a yagna without his wife, I still wanted someone to tell me it was possible. But how could even Lord Rama, my dear Rama, even think of performing a yagna when I am not in his place? Did he marry someone else? When the question of impossibility exists surrounding this ritual, how on earth would Rama actually perform it? Will there be any way out of this long tradition? As I test my memory, there is no way out of this problem, which is what my father, mother, my dear mother-in-law, and people in Mithila and Ayodhya have discussed.

My heart is still unable to picture Rama in a negative light. My mind may be correct, but my heart is not ready to accept it. I cannot believe that my Rama will perform the yagna with his new wife. Apart from getting an answer from my memory, intelligence and the saint, I now wanted to know it from the mind of a common woman. Will she have some other narrative to offer? Maybe, she would. I want to know from her that, yes! There is a way out.

Summing up considerable courage, the courage I have been living since Rama abandoned me and with which I have brought up my children bravely and obediently. I have summed up everything that I have endured through these many years. I have got the courage to walk to a woman who is busy with her daily routine. Without much ado, I took the first step, went, and I asked by interrupting her work confidently.

"Mother, I apologize for disturbing your work. I have one small question."

"Yes, you can ask. No apologies for that."

"Mother, did any king you know perform any ritual without his wife beside him?" I asked pretty impatiently.

Quite harshly and with some sense of temper, she replied, "Impossible. Bachelor or a king without his wife is not even eligible to utter the ritual's name." Deeply perturbed by her reply, I have no other way to know. I have no one else to clear my doubt. She immediately questioned, "But why are you asking me?"

For which I have no answer to reply. Deeply disturbed by the news the men from Ayodhya had got, hiding my feelings, I rushed to shed the tears that I had contained within myself since morning. I could not vent my feelings, and I now had to rush to my abode, to cry out so loudly that Rama would hear my deepest cry and stop the yagna. He should know that I am waiting for him, he should know that he has his dear Sita thinking about him, and marrying another woman for the sake of yagna is utterly wrong.

When it was entirely against the status quo of the society, just because some men in the city doubted me, he abandoned his wife to set the state right; now, what is he doing? Is Rama doing the right thing? If what I did was considered wrong, even what he is doing should also be considered unfair. But who will question this? It is Ram-Rajya, and everything in accordance with him would go right. I am feeling exhausted now with the kind of decision Rama might have taken.

***

But still, somewhere deep down in my heart, I feel that Rama would not do that. Only when Valmiki Maharshi visits Ayodhya can I ask him about the ritual's status. Until then, I have no option left to even think about it. Much to my surprise, I also visualize Rama wearing the same attire he wore during our wedding. Imagining seeing myself as the beautiful bride sitting next to him, I looked at the same visualization with keenness. But much to my surprise, I saw the same beautiful saree stoned with precious jewels. I could not wait any longer to stare at my face. With such contentedness, I looked to grab the sight of the face.

As I started to see the apparition, I felt a bit unconscious. It's not me. It's not me that Rama is marrying. Who is she? Who is she? Then is it true that Rama is marrying a woman for the yagna. Did my mother-in-law Kausalya give all my jewels to her? Leave Rama, who might be very much in need of marrying for the sake of people, but what happened to Kausalya? I have spent endless nights discussing with her. I felt her as my mother. I have spent most of my time debating with her than with my mother, Sunaina. I cannot do anything but cry.

Even cry is a small word for the level of sorrow and pain I am dealing with. But what else can I do?

Whom am I to blame? Should I blame the people? Should I blame Ravana for being the cause of all these? Or should I blame myself for crossing the limiting line Lakshmana drew? Blame? No, I do not like to be a part of the blame game. I do not want anybody to take control of my life. I will be the maker of my destiny. Let me not blame.

But suddenly, all these thoughts stopped entering my mind. I am not able to feel myself. I am unable to see anyone. Everything around me appears blank and dark. I do not know what happened all of a sudden. I am experiencing some changes in my body and soul. It feels as if someone is pulling my soul off my body. But it can never be death. No, why will I die just because of this little grief? I have faced pain beyond this, and I have overcome it strongly. I can never believe it. How can I even die without even saying a final goodbye to my kids? How will I lose my life without even seeing my dear Rama for one last time? How will I leave the earth abruptly by breaking the promise I gave to my mother, Bhudevi? Please, someone help; my soul is separated finally. I can feel some fresh air touching me.

My soul is travelling somewhere above the hermitage. I am getting an ariel view of the complete hermitage. I am trying very much to return to my own body lying down somewhere. But some force is driving me much harder to the top. I am now much above the clouds, going beyond, somewhere. I am travelling to such an altitude that I cannot see which direction I am driving.

But at once, I have been pulled down. It feels like I have been thrown from a tall mountain into the river. I am travelling down. Did God Yama think he made a mistake by taking my life and decided to bring me down to the world? Oh Yama, thank you so much for accepting my wish and bringing me down to the earth.

But no, this is not the hermitage. I am lowered down to a completely different place. But no, this is not hermitage. I just wanted to go back to the hermitage. I wanted to meet my children and be there. On this unknown journey, I do not know how to stop myself from going down here. My internal capacity is not working. Some external force is working hard and harshly upon me that I cannot escape. What is that? Where am I being taken to?

I tried to pull back my entire memory to identify the places I could see. The more down I travel, the clearer I can witness. But what is this? Something unbelievable is happening? The gopuram and the art on it appear familiar to me. Is this the same gopuram I went along with Rama the first time I came here? Looks surreal? Yes, it is. How can I forget such memorable days? Yes, I am being shifted to Ayodhya. But why?

By the time I gave my mind the space to think of my next thoughts, I was here, taken deep down to the entrance of the massive building in Ayodhya. None of the guards is stopping me. Not even one, I can see everyone, but none of them is paying attention to me.

Am I brought invisible? But why am I invisible? Did Valmiki Maharshi hear my inner voice, my pain? Did he also hear the blame game and unable to posit Rama in the blame game, did he send me to look at the ground reality and understand that my thoughts are baseless? I hope this is the intention. I hope that Valmiki did not do it to teach me some lesson.

I have started entering the court. I am not seeing anyone. The court almost looks empty. But it's pretty ridiculous to witness Ayodhya in such a manner. It is much against my expectations. I thought I would see Ayodhya in pomp and grandeur and the new queen.

But before all this, my heart is pumping the blood faster and beating with so much pressure. Now that I have got the chance to come to Ayodhya, everything flew away. I started forgetting about the yagna. Nothing is hitting my mind except the dream, which was almost impossible to even think of. The dream that I have partially fulfilled is through the eyes of my two sons, who have seen Rama and Ayodhya. But even with them, I cannot ask anything except if Rama is good. Anything beyond that question would raise suspicion. I did not have a good encounter with them as they misunderstood Rama. What else can I even think? Now crossing all of this, I have the chance to see my Rama with my own eyes. My heart started desperately searching for my dear Rama. But much to my surprise, I saw something like a statue covered with a cloth. Quickly noticing that no one was there around me, I uncovered the fabric.

I received a tremendous shock at the moment. For some time, I could not quite believe what I saw.

***

It was an immensely decorated Sita's statue in gold. It's my statue, quite unbelievable. Now I understood how Rama wanted to do the ritual. It's not by getting married to a queen, but he made me in gold, and the golden Sita will sit in place of me. Perhaps he is the first man in the entire clan to make a golden statue of his wife, just for the sake of people. This one image has brought the entire thoughts into control.

It seems I am going to put dristi to it. It has almost everything, but only one thing is found missing. It is the Chandra tilak underneath the bindi that Rama loves the most.

Quickly taking my vermillion, I applied it onto the statue, and as I did that, I noticed someone coming in my way. I want it to be Rama, and yes, after more than ten years, I see my dear Rama with my own naked eyes. It's an unbelievable feeling that I am even finding words short of expressing them.

He has come. And as soon as he entered, he just spoke only one word. "Sita! Sita! Sita! Are you here?" I am quite sure I am invisible, but how on earth was Rama able to find my presence? Maybe this is what true love is. Impeccable to even think about. This is why people adore Rama. This is perhaps the reason why people call him the perfect man. Who on earth would even get the idea to make a wife's statue in gold for the yagna, and who would do such a great act? I am intrigued, and Rama is making me fall in love again and again with his deeds. Just a glance into his eyes is enough to see how much he still loves me. Now I do not even care if my soul goes back to the hermitage or directly to heaven or hell.

And suddenly he started talking to me. Something which I never thought about.

"Sita! See how much I am sorrow-stricken. Even though I know you are chaste, I have abandoned you to the deep wilderness just for the sake of good rule. I might have committed some grievous crime in my previous birth to make you go through such troubles. Will I even get to see you, Sita, in this birth? Not just this birth, even in my next births in the future."

As Rama is talking to my statue, it is as if he is conversing with me straightforwardly. He started crying, but I can also see another face. Yes, my son Lava. Lava also looks the same way when crying. But now, it's tough for me to see Rama crying in this manner.

He should always be standing still, in a gracious posture; seeing him like this, his tears stooping him down, is unbearable. He at once collapsed down near my statue and started to look at my statue's face. He who looked so much dull, so much sorrowful, at once looked at the statue's face and stood up straight. It felt as if he got some instant energy, but what happened? What's there in my face?

To know what happened, why did my dear Rama look at the apparition and felt some instant energy passing through him? I looked at the apparition clearly and noticed his favorite vermillion that I had put. He knows very clearly that no one else knows about that. It was more like a secret that stayed only between us. Is Rama going to doubt that I have come here? Who else will he even think has put the vermillion?

He is now overjoyed and started crying, "Sita! Sita!" Initially, the voice did not come out that well because the pain was a barrier to his voice. Now it appears as if he is screaming at the top of his voice. The joy has motivated him to pronounce my name with utmost happiness. I am falling in love with Rama.

This vermillion that I have put beneath my bindi appears to be a metaphor for our love. Before, the Shiva's bow proved our love and helped us come together, but now this vermillion is acting as the agent to show how much Rama loves me. This vermillion secret was kept between us more than ten years before. Even though I was absent in Ayodhya, living some miles apart from Rama. Still, it is Rama's greatness to remember everything, even being busy amidst his duties as a King.

Rama's presence of mind is what makes him stand above everything. Though initially, he took my heart by breaking the Shiva's bow, as soon as I came here, he took my heart for the second time through the presence of mind he showcased. His thoughts are unmatchable. I never, even in my wildest dreams, thought that a king would make a statue out of gold in the absence of his wife. And even before I am back to reality from the previous lovely gestures from Rama, the vermillion, which when I have put, I thought would never be noticed by Rama has seen the unnoticeable.

Now I clearly understand why everybody loves Rama and is considered unique. The feeling of guilt is flowing like a stream inside my heart. I have done what can never be done by any wife. That day, without knowing Rama's intention, I wept so hard to Lakshman, and it took time to correct myself. Many of such thoughts used to visit me every day. They grew more and more when I was utterly unbearable with the fact that Rama was performing a yagna without me. And hence, unable to withhold this vagueness and curiosity, I have asked some people in the hermitage. Unable to witness his favourite person being put to constant questioning, Valmiki, through his cognitive power, would have sent me here.

My Rama makes my world. I do not need anything else in life. Even though I was at the hermitage, my thoughts always stayed with Rama. Now, it feels that I have got everything in my life. Ranging from my kids, I have brought them up in a commendable manner, teaching them in the best possible way, making them learn the value of relationships, the need to overthrow war, and saving lives. I have taught them more than a single mother could teach, and I am proud of them.

On the other hand, I am satisfied that Rama is also ruling the country with no discrepancies. On my way to Ayodhya, I heard people speaking positively about Rama's rule here at Ayodhya. Everyone is happy and poverty is almost eradicated. Is there anything else in life that a wife can feel satisfied with rather than having a good ruler beyond a good husband and good sons like their father?

My heart is filled with joy. Some sense of completeness is wrapping me around. Even if I return to the hermitage, I do not feel about Rama hereafter. I am looking at my dear Rama deeply, and I want to fill my entire heart with his image to live the rest of my life. As I started staring at his face, I could not even hear what he was speaking. I am just living the moment, as people say. I am still staring at how Rama is not just containing the joy within himself but expressing it out loud. It now feels as if now I am seeing Kusha in his face. How does it look when the person who does not laugh most of the time is primarily silent and does not express his views to others? He, who cannot be understood at the very first instance, now smiles and expresses himself, this is Kusha. He looks the same way Kusha is smiling and expressing his joy.

He started caressing my statue and is roaming in the court, pronouncing my name Sita, Sita, with more of such depth. I am standing here, looking at his excitement, scared to see him like this. I am afraid that everyone who never saw Rama in this position will question him hard about what has happened. I am also standing here quite worried. Will Valmiki lift my soul from here? No, I want to stay for some more time. I want to look at my mother-in-law. Please, I started praying inside. What else can I do now? Nothing is in my control unless I unite with my body.

Rama is walking unsteadily, looking for me. He is still screaming my name out very loud. The effect of which his voice will not work for a few days.

I just wanted to hold my Rama's hands and tell him not to worry, I am here, and my soul will be here in Ayodhya, with you. I also wanted to tell the secret about his sons. Even though my emotional mind is ruling on the top, my intellectual or logical mind is still controlling. If not, I would have tried many ways to convey the truth to Rama.

But I do not know how and where this will end. Rama, please be patient. Rama, please come back to normal. I do not want people to judge you as a lunatic. I know you love me, and you long for me so much. You know I am present here, but you cannot convince the people around you that I have been here. This is my internal prayer to Rama, deep inside, so deep that Rama would hear my thoughts and act in a dignified manner. I now closed my eyes and started to feel the sentences until they reached Rama. His love for me is dominating my words. The more I prayed inside, the more he screamed out very loud.

And at once, I heard the sound, bang! Rama has fallen near the statue, still calling out my name. Oh,

God! Please help, my dear Rama. Seeing him in this condition is not making me happy.

To stop his sorrows, I went and touched his forehead. I thought he wouldn't recognize my touch. Again, much to my surprise, he started saying, "Yes, yes. This is Sita's touch."

I am pleased to touch my Rama after these long years, which felt like some yugas. No one else can understand the pain Rama's separation has got, likewise, no one can imagine how contained I am with Rama's touch. His forehead seems so dull. And I can feel the amount of pain he is going through. But cannot help.

"Devi, Devi, you have come. Devi! Devi! You have come. Did it take you these many years to show some concern for me? Devi, Devi", he cried.

Unknown of how this conversation would extend, I drew my hand back and took blessings in the air.

Restricting and constraining myself from such activities sounded the need of the hour for me. I was surprised to know I could move as I wished. Now I am flying on my terms, which I did not expect. "Rama, Rama, Rama," at once, I was at the top of Ayodhya, wishing a final goodbye to the place as I am unknown of the journey I am still to take and the destiny that I am to face. I went as swiftly as possible, but still the voice of Rama shouting with pain as Sita! Sita! is still resonating in my mind. My heart and eyes are filled, not leaving space for air to travel, disturbing the momentum of Rama's image.

With the kind of emotion Rama is in, definitely now his mother Kausalya would have come and asked him about the happening. It's good if Rama abstains from telling them that Sita has come because no matter what he explains, they are not going to believe. Only the pure love existing between persons would make all these things possible and now these acts of being able to talk between ourselves without even being able to see each other is divine experience or divine bliss.

Rama, please take care of the kingdom well and don't forget to take care of yourself before you think of the kingdom. Wishing him, I have swiftly entered my body.

***

Slowly, as soon as I woke up, I saw Valmiki Maharshi sitting on the chair, and I was at once shocked. The first word he uttered was "Doubt. Sita, never doubt your Rama. Never doubt the love of Rama, Sita. Don't doubt Raghuram's love."

I know. I feel guilty for the act of doubt. I understood it only after going there and witnessing Rama's condition.

"Sita Mata! Rama can kill any enemy how much soever he is great with one arrow. If he has given any word, he will never break it, and he will work very hard to keep that word, no matter how harsh the consequences are. Likewise, Rama's love will be vested only upon one woman. Please do not doubt your Rama, Sita!" said Valmiki.

My heart is shrinking with Valmiki's words.

"Even if the sky breaks down and falls, he will never disobey his vow. So please don't doubt Rama's love, Sita."

I could not stop my tears.

"If Rama has left his dharma and loves another woman, not just my chant, but the epic I have written will go into nothing. Please don't doubt Rama, Sita Mata," said Valmiki.

"Swami, My God, my Sree Rama, I made such a big mistake by doubting Rama, my Rama. How cruel, how wicked I am. Is there anything that I can do to clean up my act of doubt? Please, Swami.

"Please tell me. I want to purify myself from the negative thoughts I have made." I requested Valmiki.

My heart is feeling very heavy due to this mistake. "Please, Swami, is there anything I can do?" I asked Valmiki again.

I have committed a grave mistake by doubting my husband. But I can't help. If your husband has abandoned you without even informing , sends his brother to drop you off and thence you get to know about it through him, unknown of your future as a woman, unknown of your future as a wife, unknown of your future as a mother, unknown of your existence at the outmost, and you grow stronger bravely, you grow even stronger by looking at your sons resembling their father and being devoid of any such news from Ayodhya before, now at once you hear news that devastates you completely, shatters the hope of not your future but the children's future, the information that the king is going to perform a yagna, and you have been taught till now that a king cannot perform yagna in the absence of his wife, but your heart even then wants to negate this particular statement and thereby you go asking people about some limitations to the yagna being performed without a wife and you receive all the responses in a negative manner, none to share grief with, not with a father like Valmiki Maharshi, and cannot not be with sons like Lava and Kusha, what can you do at the most? Doubt that your husband might go for marriage for the sake of good society. Isn't it? Because that is all, you are left with.

After seeing my dear Rama's love for me and looking through my own naked eyes, I hate myself. Beyond all of this, Valmiki's questions have struck me like an arrow, so deep into my heart that I feel as if I would give up my life with excessive bleeding. Valmiki Maharshi would have felt so worried about me doubting Rama in this manner. If not, he would not send me on such an impossible ride to even think about.

I want to purify myself for this horrendous error that I have committed. I have to ask Maharshi anything I can do to take over this doubt. Will there be any task that I can do to overcome this?

"Maharshi, will there be any ritual I can perform to purify the sin that I have committed?" I asked Valmiki.

"Sita Mata, never call the doubt you have committed, a sin. It's normal to think like that in unusual circumstances."

"Swami, it's not like that. Even committing a crime mentally towards my dear Rama is a huge mistake…My inner peace will never be at stake if you do not say."

Maharshi thinks that doubting Rama in such a manner is not a mistake. I understand that he knows in what situation and context I have done. It might be a usual scenario in the light of a relationship between an ordinary man and woman. Still, I am not performing a self-appraisal of myself but expressing it by foregrounding Rama's characteristics as a husband. To such a king like Rama, the thought of doubt is also a huge error. This is the reason behind standing very much on my word even when Valmiki Maharshi has tried convincing me that I have not committed the crime.

With the limited verbal conversation exchanges we have made between ourselves, Valmiki Maharshi on the one hand and I on the other, finally unable to see the pain flushing through my eyes, Valmiki Maharshi has taken a deep breath. He has gone into a temporary meditation state. Seeing this gesture, I took a deep breath and eagerly awaited a prompt solution from Valmiki Maharshi.

He is still thinking about some calculations. With the passage of every second, my anxiety is doubling. I want to do some redemption practice, basically for my satisfaction. Unless performed, I would again get back into the loop of endless thoughts bashing my mind, leaving no peace in my work, maintaining a healthy relationship with my kids, or with my sleep. I thereby am waiting so eagerly like a kid waiting for their mother.

All of a sudden, I started sweating, maybe due to the pressure I was giving on my mind, or this might be the result of constantly looking at Valmiki Maharshi's eyes as to when they would open. But, as the place was so calm, I suddenly heard the noises of Lava and Kusha coming back from the gurukul. My heart started beating fast. I do not, at any cost, want them to know about this. This would be so much of an insult to me as a dutiful mother.

This time, my eyes are not just focused on Valmiki Maharshi's meditative state but also on the entrance of the house. My eyes are looking beyond the house's entrance to spot them as quickly as possible so that it would provide me with an escape to refrain them from involving in this horrendous activity.

As I noticed both corners, I found Valmiki Maharshi gesturing something in the air. He should be calculating something related to the redemption act. And now, opening his eyes, he started staring at the distant sky, and by uttering a few shlokas, he called my name, "Sita Mata."

"Maharshi…", I said.

"Sita Mata, for your mental peace, to forbid all the sins and to fulfil your desires, there is a vrat that you have to follow."

"Ah! Listening to this feels like a calm sea, without any waves, and a rainy night without massive winds and thunders. I eagerly await the kind of vrat I will be doing. But again, my heart kept pounding. Will the vrat Maharshi say, can it be doable or include some complications to follow? No, this time, I have very quickly negated my mind saying, never Valmiki does not give me the task one cannot perform. Taking a deep breath, and with much positivity, I am just waiting to hear Valmiki's reply, with such excitement that I will start it right quickly in a matter of seconds.

"Mother Sita! Perform the deeksha for nine days and worship Jaganmata Lalitha Devi with lotus flowers. This is the right vrat to perform. You must be very particular about this and do it manasa, vacha, karmena. That means your mind, speech and actions should be completely focused on the yagna you are about to perform. Sitamma, you already have done many vrat in your life before. There is nothing much I could say, but you must be diligent in performing this vrat."

"Swami, I will follow your advice and suggestions."

"But…" Valmiki stopped saying something.

Are there any complications, again?

I was waiting with thousand eyes for swami to listen to the continuation, but hoping that does not again set the limit for the vrat I just wanted to perform. I am paying complete attention to the 'but' that Valmiki Maharshi has just stopped. He is currently taking some time. I do not understand why. Is there anything serious, or is there something he is finding hard to say? Should I interrupt his speech and ask? Or will it not be nice to ask a Maharshi like him about this aspect? Should I or should I not? Should I wait for him to complete his speech? My heart interrupted my strategic thinking and said that you had waited so long, and there was nothing wrong with waiting for five more minutes. Let Maharshi take his own time. He knows when to do and when not to.

I am waiting endlessly.

"Sita Mata! But, there is one strong condition or limitation to this, which you should never violate in any instance. If you violate it at any time of your yagna everything you have been performing would be of utter waste. You have to understand one thing very clearly. The more important the task is, the more complicated it will be. Only passing through tests like these, you would be stepping into the divine realm of eternal happiness", said Valmiki.

"Yes, Maharshi." I nodded, this time not with an emotional slumber but quite confidently. So that I want my gesture to notify Maharshi that I am serious about this vrat, and I would do it with manas ekam, vachas ekam and karmana yekam.

Satisfied with the reply that I have put through the gesture, Valmiki Maharshi has proceeded.

"Even if the world is against it, trying to stop you, even if you get to know that there is something important that you should cater to, or even if there is some impending danger, Listen carefully. You should never stop the vrat in the middle. This is the only condition that you should follow. If it happens, it would only be a problem to you, Sita Mata."

"Swami. I will never let it stop in between, at any instance. But Swami, I have one query. Who would bring me the lotus that you have just mentioned? Are they rare, or will they be found deep in the forests?"

Amidst all of a sudden, I heard some sound that seemed to be coming from the entrance. The tone sounds very familiar. I wonder if they are my sons, as a mother never fails to recognize the voice of her sons, wherever they are. Lava and Kusha would have come. To confirm, I immediately glanced at the entrance without expecting a reply from Valmiki Maharshi.

Yes, Lava and Kusha are back from gurukul. They would have indulged in after-school playtime activities with their friends, as I have heard them coming near to me long before, and it took time for them to come over here. Their friend circle has grown enormously these days. More than Kusha, Lava is turning out to be naughty. I only doubt what if they have listened to the entire conversation by hiding behind the entrance. I want to make it clear.

Meanwhile, with so much affection, Lava came near Maharshi and took his blessings. Following this, Kusha also did the same. Then they both took my blessings.

"Mother, do not worry. We are there to get that specific kind of lotus flowers you were saying to Guru."

"Mother, not just these flowers, you name anything, we would find and put them in your hands in the wink of an eye. Please do not be worried about where to find it. We would ask Maharshi to tell us about where they are. We will find them and get them for you."

Listening to these words. I am relaxed. They did not listen to our entire conversation. If they have heard it, they would ask me what that yagna is and why I am performing this yagna would be their first question.

Valmiki Maharshi hugged Lava and Kusha, "When you have kids like these two, what else do you need in life, Sita Mata?"

Talking to Kusha, Valmiki Maharshi spoke, "My Kusha, for your mother's vrat, you must get those flowers."

At once, Lava questioned Valmiki Maharshi with so much intensity, "Guruvarya, to help my mother, is my brother the only eligible one, and am I not?"

This is where Lava differs from me. If I have questions I need to ask elders like Valmiki Maharshi, I would think twice or thrice. I would end up not even asking the doubt and staying silent as a sign of respect, but the kind of question Lava has outrightly asked Valmiki Maharshi is making me raise my eyebrows. In this aspect, he behaves like his father, Rama, who is not scared of anyone. If he has anything to ask, he will not step back and would do it without a second thought, and Lava has developed the same aspect.

Usually, Valmiki Maharshi assigns the task to both of them equally. He does not show any level of bias in this. But if he had pointed out that only one could perform the task, there would be a strong purpose behind it.

"Dear Lava, please come here. You uttered a big word. Don't I know your love for your mother? But, why will I, and who am I to forbid you from this divine task? You have got some other tasks to do, and thence I am abstaining you from this activity. Listen very carefully. Today I have to go to Bharadwaj's ashram; until I come, it will be your task to take care of the ashram completely. Be very alert when doing this; you must protect every nook and corner of the ashram. Hope you understood, what I mean, Lava." Bowing his head in complete reverence, Lava has agreed to fulfil his duty.

With this, Valmiki Maharshi took leave, and Lava started,

"My dear brother Kusha, did you listen to what Valmiki Maharshi has just told? Or was your concentration somewhere else? I think you did not listen to what Maharshi said as you were standing somewhere far from Valmiki Maharshi. He said that it is my duty to safeguard the ashram. And you can happily go to collect all the essential things needed for the vrat, be careful when you are collecting the flowers, and you need to do it at any cost. Maharshi is going to take the leave, and it again becomes my duty and responsibility to take care that the vrat goes safely. I am younger than you, but I have been bestowed with such a huge task compared to others", said Lava with pride in his eyes.

***

Kusha knows that his task of collecting the flowers, which he has never seen or heard so far, is going to be more adventurous than chanting the shlokas, singing the huge Ramayana composition, or going for archery. He knows it is for a greater purpose, so Maharshi has assigned him this role. Even though Lava is committed to his work, Maharshi knows well that if he finds something exciting in the middle or meets someone mid-way who challenges him, he would prioritize his self-attitude and leave the work in between. Kusha knows what his brother is, and to avoid further discussion, he says, "Lava, my brother, yes, that is a commendable task that you have. I do not know why Valmiki Maharshi did not give me such a huge task of protecting the ashram. But Lava, as I venture out into the deep forests and mountains, I am vesting it in your hands to take care of our dear mother and the ashram simultaneously."

Interrupting Kusha's speech, Lava says, "My dear brother, please correct me if I am wrong, this is what Valmiki Maharshi has told me, and as you have stressed it again, even by putting my very own life on the trail, I would perform this task. You will only see soon how Lava's protection would be. Are you ready to be protected by Lava, the great?"

Outrightly restricting himself from any other dialogue so that it would not prolong any unwanted and unnecessary conversation, with a huge smile on his face, Kusha hugged Lava, "Dear Lava, I am so very proud of you; I wish you all the very best for your role."

"I wish you the same wholeheartedly, brother," said Lava to Kusha.

Both hugged one another, and after all the dialogues between themselves, they realized that I was there, still standing. As if I am standing at the end of the running race, and would be giving them some gift for the one who finishes the race first, came running faster and hugged me.

"Mother. Forgive us for making you stand this long. We completely forgot about everything as we were busy debating."

By taking blessings, they quickly hurried for their dinner. It was a long day for them today. We all would be wholly occupied with the ritual starting tomorrow for about nine days. As suggested by Valmiki Maharshi, I should be ready to sacrifice my complete self in the coming nine days. Kusha would be immersed in his adventurous roller-coaster ride of collecting the flowers for the ritual. Lava would be even more occupied with his daily schedule, pretending to be the monarch of the entire hermitage. So, I think it is ideal if we can all sit together and talk for some time.

Though we have been doing everyday discussions ever since they started to go to the gurukul, after immersing themselves in the archery and Ramayana singing composition, we did not have enough time to catch up. So, after we all had our dinner, I would usually just let them sleep with a story from my side. Lava takes one to two minutes to sleep, while Kusha would hum till I complete the entire story. I went tip-toed to their sleeping place. Both are fully covered because of the winter blows.

I stood by their side for some time to check if they had slept, patiently waiting to see if they would make at least a slight movement. I stood there for almost five minutes, but I did not see the slightest movement. Convinced that the two kids would be exhausted after a long day. I silently tip-toed to my place to do little work for tomorrow's event.

"Mother…" I heard a slight noise, like Lava's voice. So happy to find them still awake, I quickly looked at their place. Still, I did not find any movement. Then, with a little more disappointment that it would just be my hallucination, I heard the voice again. But this time completely fixed that it's again my obsession. I was going back, finding for some object.

Then at once, I felt that someone is following me back. I could sense the sound. But as I turned around, I did not find any. I proceeded further, thinking that my hallucination had travelled deep down to my mind.

This time I heard the slightest laughter that Lava usually makes. But I thought. "Sita, calm down. Enough of what you have been doing for half an hour. It's time now to sleep and walk up early. Think of Rama, and everything would go fine now." My inner urge has dominated me so much that it did not even give me a second to think of the sound behind me. Then, I searched for an object; I had stopped searching before.

"Woosh." At once, Lava and Kusha came from behind and wrapped their hands around my hip. Thank God, I thought I had some neurotic disorder for a while.

Before I could even shout for playing silly tricks at night time, Lava and Kusha at once pecked kisses on my cheeks and together, "Mother, we are extremely sorry for making fun of you at this serious moment. Every day you would make us sleep by narrating beautiful stories. You even sing for us sometimes. But I thought we would have some fun with you for a change. We have planned something bigger, but your expressions made us rethink our plan. As we have seen you standing near us constantly looking at us for five minutes and then the disappointment levels that we have noticed, mother, made us surrender way before in advance", they said.

The reason behind their plan and the way they defended their fun was mind-blowing. These two are growing faster in their intellect. I should also evolve according to their mentality; if not, they will dominate me.

I caressed their hair and made them sit down. We sat down, looking at the fresh sky with stars hiding behind the clouds. The trees seem to be all frozen due to the winter season. Usually, we hear few animal sounds, but today, all the animals seem to be in their hibernation mode. The forest is pitch dark, with not even the slightest sound and slightest movement. The external environment also made us reduce our volume so that our noise won't disturb the surrounding people in the ashram.

"Mother, you seem so anxious with a little tension. Is it because of the ritual that is to begin tomorrow? But, do not worry, mother, we will do our best to make it successful. But why are you performing the ritual, mother? Is there any reason behind it?" asked Lava.

Lava has finally put the most expected question I have been thinking about since they heard about this ritual. He outrightly questioned Valmiki Maharshi yesterday, and I thought he would ask if there is any strong reason behind this ritual. And now the question has come up.

"Listen, Lava; firstly, I have to say something important. You both have to listen and follow it very carefully. If a person is doing any good work and is about to start, you should appreciate it but should never ask why before it. Good things do not need a why behind them. And anyone who is actually performing a yagna would be doing it not just for their own good but also for the common good of the world. I think you also have got the answer to your question."

"Yes, mother. Hereafter we would never ask why before any good thing."

"So, Lava and Kusha, how is your school going?" I asked.

"Mother, this week at the gurukul, apart from learning the shlokas, archery, and astras, we were also given the task of cleaning our surroundings. Indulging in this stressful work is taking most of our energy. You would have thought we are playing with our friends after school hours and hence we are coming home tired. But this is the reason, mother. Due to this, we also got several friends with whom we spent time discussing new topics and sharing knowledge. But, mother, usually you would sit out and watch our performances in the school. But we have not seen you these days, mother. Seems you are busy with some work, mother."

How can I tell them what has changed my daily schedule? Ever since the soldiers from Ayodhya came, my heart and mind were not in my control.

You all know how much I was suffering with the innumerable thoughts, even the most nonsensical ones that troubled me. I do not want to get into that again in my life. Even though the ritual I am performing now will not let me reveal the reason behind it. I will try not to think about it. I have to stop thinking about it now.

I have shown them something moving in the sky to distract them for a while. But after examining it for a bit, I knew it was a comet. It was moving at such a great speed, and they were stunned at the kind of brightness. It's as if the star is making the entire cloud bright, sharing its shine; as the proverbial saying goes, "Every cloud has its silver lining." And as every cloud has a silver lining, even every problem has a positive side. Though Valmiki Maharshi has given a temporary solution to the problem that I am facing, that is, the yagna, I still doubt that this will end up somewhere else.

Maybe this is why we are going for an unusual discussion at night. God, the ultimate, shows some prior hints in life. My thoughts never deceived me, except the last time I doubted Rama. Nature has demonstrated wrong signs through the disappearance of the mother bird in the nest, the unnatural act of Rama's sleep, the environment around, Lakshmana's silence, and again this time, Lava and Kusha's Ayodhya trip ended with their hatred towards Rama for abandoning Sita.

I am sensing something wrong again today. But, as a result of everything I have experienced so far, the only aspect I learnt is not to think of the future that might happen somewhere later. I have determined to live happily in the present.

After being banished, I can say life has been a good teacher. Maybe this is why people say you learn and grow when you are alone. When I first entered the ashram, I was a bit skeptical. Mother Bhumi guarded me before I was found by King Janak while ploughing the land for the yagna and later on protected by King Janak. After getting married to Lord Rama, you all know I could not even spend a few minutes without Rama being by my side. This was the sole reason behind following Rama to the vanavas, even though I didn't need to go to exile.

From a point where I thought I could not live without Rama to a point where I have raised my kids as a single mother, this is beyond my hope or what has been re-instated in my mind ever since I was a child, that a girl cannot live without male support, be it father or husband or son.

Hence, my dear young daughters or sisters or mothers, I have the lesson that never lose hope; when life hits you very hard, smile and keep going.

And secondly, as I have already told you, never let the thoughts disturb your mental peace. Always remember to find peace within yourselves and not externally. Never let the thoughts disturb your mental stability as they did mine. I have struggled with my thoughts; I do not want to repeat them. As you have travelled with me throughout, you know what constant thoughts did to me and made me.

Today, I want to let you know that just like the cloud with the silver lining, remember to find positive things amidst all the negative aspects that life does to you. And thoughts are always meant to enter your mind. Never let them enter your heart; stop them at the earliest. If not, your mental peace will be at stake.

I thought all these lessons I have learnt from my own experiences would be helpful to know them way before and develop. But I can guess your inner feeling. Because when my mother, Queen Sunaina, was explaining the same life lessons from her life, I did not pay any attention and was thinking just because she had faced such trouble did not mean that I would also be going through the same. But only later did I come to know that with problems, only when we experience them personally would we connect the dots. Taking my suggestions would make your life less troublesome.

Today, beyond being a proud daughter to my father and dutiful wife to my dear Rama, I love to be called a proud mother to my sons, Lava, and Kusha. As a daughter and wife, I have been influenced by many people around me. But as a mother, right from taking care of them in my womb, I know when they are hungry, I know how to cheer them up when they are silent, I know how to share happiness with them, I know their needs, only I, a mother knows. They have become mine ultimately. Whatever they have learnt or their attitude towards life, everything is mine. But I shall not control or overpower them.

I know the limiting point of my role as a mother. Hence, I would start taking the role of a friend to advise them, and once I reach the zenith, I would stop there. This is the first piece of advice to all the mothers out there. Let them take time to develop and give enough space to find their interests. Do not overshadow them. It woke me up. I completely forgot about what my children were doing. They were conversing and laughing their hearts out. Lying on the floor, they are gazing at the sky by putting their hands below their head. It's been so long since I saw them talking together without arguing or performing a word war.

"Lava Kusha! Lava Kusha! Lava Kusha!" I have called them thrice, but they are unresponsive. It's as if they have blocked all the noise. Let them be in their own world, I thought.

Without disturbing them much, I started to enjoy nature. The winter smell we experience when it clubs with the scent of the leaves or flowers nearby works like a chemical reaction, they both lose part of their fragrance and come together with a different smell. Flowers and the winter created a new fragrance. The greenery clubbed with the darkness around is making my eyes feel afresh. My ears are resting due to the muteness of the environment that nature created, my nose is just busy experiencing the beautiful reaction smell, and my sense of touch is experiencing the cool breeze.

I feel as if nature has overtaken control of my entire body. After many painful and stressful days, I feel my body light. It seems like I do not have any pressure on me. As sages say, when people reach far heights in the sky, they can feel it as zero gravity, where if you do not feel the pressure of your entire body, the universe will bear you, and you are all left to be free.

We tend to neglect our physique and our psyche or sometimes over care one another due to our busy schedule or routine rooted in our everyday life. Occasionally, we pay attention to our minds through various mental exercises like meditation. At the same time, we often just focus on the physical body by doing physical workouts like walking and household chores.

Men require physical strength and mental ability to check on the enemy as they go out for the war. People say it is an equally challenging task. On the other hand, they mock women saying you sit at home and do not need much mental agility to work; just physical strength would help.

Even though I was taught this in school, the scenario at home rather than at the palace was completely different. I have seen my father, King Janak, giving equal attention to Queen Sunaina regarding state matters. Queen Sunaina also has her part in King Janak's decisions. I have also heard of

King Janak as the first supporter of women and women's rights. Even sometimes council of ministers used to doubt the king's decision by saying, "Dear Janak, the decision seems a bit perplexing. Maybe you would have decided upon it because of some influence. Please take a relook at your decision." King Janak answered, "I even choose my influencers acting upon me so their decisions won't be wrong. You need not worry about it. You have to go with the decisions I have put before you all." King Janak knows that the people are very perplexed by the kind of value and respect he showers upon women.

Hence, they always try to demean it by making King Janak understand that women are meant only for physical chores, and their mental ability will not be that much in a good place to decide. My father told me only two things, "Firstly, a woman, if thrown into a place where she cannot but depend on herself, should be mentally agile to take care of herself. Secondly, she should always learn the skills usually taught to men. Even though she might not use those at any point in their life, she should learn them. We do not know what trouble might behest upon her at a later point of time."

These words came true as my mental strength has helped me overcome troubles and care for myself. And, as when I grew up in my place, my father taught me various skills, which also helped me now after my sons are born, by becoming their first teacher and helping them grow right from home.

As I was completely immersed in my thoughts, a huge thunder made me aware that even Lava and Kusha exist apart from my own self. And with this, they also left their long or deep or magical conversation, came running towards me and hugged out the scary sound that nature made. This is quite different weather. Initially, it was such cool pleasant weather, where nature was very still, my thoughts were flying high, and kids were both doing the perfect weather chatting. Now, the leaves started moving, the trees are swinging, and it feels as if they have found their new bound freedom, which the winter has restricted.

I bet the trees would be muttering or whispering between themselves. They would have had a tough time due to their uncontrollable abstinence from their friends. But today, they have regained their lost freedom. They would just have waited for this moment in their life to rejoin their friends. Breeze has become their releaser of prison created by winter. We experienced with our friends that if we were restricted for some days, the suppressed feelings and emotions within ourselves would grow, and at once, we try to talk about our life in between.

We do not talk about all this slowly but would immediately jump on the topic. We initially try to bash out all the suppressed things, and later, we reduce our pace. It felt the same for me today. The first blow of breeze gave that kind of momentum to their lives, and the trees started bashing out, trying to stretch their branches as much as possible to shake their friend's hands. Later on, even though the breeze was high, the trees did not move in accordance with the high breeze. It feels as if their stories have finished, and they have expressed themselves completely. Now again, they are back to their routine life.

Does not it seem that I am observing nature too much? It might be because of my stay at the Panchavati, close to nature. I did not have anything else to see or view there, and even people were few except rakshasis here and there. Later on, here at Dandaka Forest, while I felt lonely, I would watch the woods to find some joy, and when I felt happy, I would still look at the forest to share my inner joy. Today was one such roller-coaster day that I have found within myself. It seems I was conversing with nature.

"Mother, mother," called Lava.

"Yes, the caretaker of the hermitage, please say," I said in a mocking tone.

"Mother, shall we please go back to sleep? It's almost late night and the thunders have begun. Please, shall we?" asked Lava.

While Lava can manage anyone on this planet, any person, or even any animal for that matter, the only thing perhaps he is scared about is the thunders. He never likes to be outside when nature is at its highest reactive state. He would love to stay indoors, cover himself up completely, especially his ears, and sleep.

"Savior of the land, you are our to be ruler. And we are your subjects. We will enact as per your wishes. We would live according to your orders." I prayed.

"Mother, stop teasing me, please. Can we please?"

I nodded my head and found Lava running inside as fast as he could. Much to my surprise, Kusha, who generally wishes to walk alone and to stand alone from the group he is part of, is holding my hand and waiting for me to step inside.

"Let's go, Kusha. We have so much in place to do from tomorrow. Let's sleep as soon as possible and have to wake up early." Kusha nodded his head.

As we went in, I found Lava in his deep sleep; without making much noise, I made Kusha sleep, patted his back, and curled my hand across his hair. I am just ensuring that, like any mother, they are both comfortable sleeping.

Tiredness is setting inside me like a ray of light through the small opening beside the main door.

***

Cockka-ro-kkoo, Cockka-ro-kkoo, Cockka-ro-kkoo, is the rooster crowing even before her time today? My mind is still so sleepy that I feel it is too early to be early morning today. Usually, my eyes open as soon as I get the consciousness that it is morning, and I would wake up at once. But today, my eyes are still sleepy, doubting if the rooster is actually on time. I tried to sleep for some more time; my heart is battling with my mind. They both appear engrossed in a terrific unimaginable duel, so much that I have given up my complete determination to sleep.

I finally woke up. It seems I have actually fought one huge war and ultimately won. But my battle did not contain any swords or some other sharp instruments; just my thoughts were playing tug-of-war. These two thoughts are sharp swords. And there is no colossal battleground for the thoughts to fight. Well, you have got it; my mind is the battleground. Proud of myself that I woke up. I went directly to check what Lava and Kusha are doing. They would not have woken up; I have taken so much time to wake up on this pitch-dark winter morning after a thunderous night. Putting my expectations right in place, I still found them very happy in their slumber. I should finish little preparations before they are awake to avoid the further delay.

Before starting my actual ritual, I took time to re-think what Valmiki Maharshi had told me about this ritual. I will have to be so much more attentive and immerse my complete self into the vrat for the best results. If not, the only chance I have to heal myself because of the guilt will take me down. With this, I proceeded to start the rituals, remembering Rama.

Rama, you know why I am doing this ritual. I have doubted the perfect human on earth, and I do not want to hold that mark for the rest of my life. And secondly, I would like Lava and Kusha to be in the best of their capacities and capabilities before they meet you.

These are my two desires behind performing the ritual. Please be there to protect us from any ill and evil. "Jai Sree Ram. Jai Sree Ram!" I heard a dual voice behind me. "Mother, look who is here."

I was surprised to see Lava and Kusha. "Why did you both wake up way ahead of your regular time?" I asked.

"Mother, we have planned to wake up early these nine days. And, as Kusha and I have new roles to play from today, we are excited and tensed equally to take care so that no mishappening would happen. Please let us know what help we can do before we go out on our duties."

"Lava and Kusha, remember one thing before setting out the tasks for you today. Today is the beginning day of the ritual, and nine days from today, please promise me that you will not fight amongst yourself and make me angry. As you know, this is a significant one, and I have to be very attentive." I told them.

"Yes, mother. Please mark our words. We swear we will not get into an argument, making you worried. We will cooperate at our best and not create any discomposure for you. Please bless us, mother."

"My blessings will always be with you, my dear sons. Not just between you two, you should also not get into a duel with any people outside." I told them.

"Mother, we will ensure our best. Now shall we please start the ritual?"

"Yes, I have some little work for you. Divide between yourselves accordingly, pull off the work by dedicating your complete self and complete it. And when you are doing it, please chant Sree Rama."

"Yes, mother." Lava and Kusha started to do the pre-ritual work, and I soon immersed myself in my task. With this, the most awaited day has finally begun.

I heard today is the divyamuhurtham to start any event. So, not just me indulging in this ritual; my conscience somewhere is striking that even Rama would be performing it. While I have started the ritual of worshipping Lalitha Devi, much to my surprise, I can visualize Rama performing Ashvamedha Yagna with the blessings of Lord Vinayaka. I feel I am there, beside him and performing.

I can also clearly visualize Ayodhya, people who have come to witness the start of the great event in history. The prayer hall in the main court is decorated with various flowers, and fresh fruits are hanging all over. While the sages were performing the yagna, pouring ghee into Agni, several courtesans graced the event with their finest performances, adding a new vibration to the yagna. It feels like the entire Ayodhya is here to witness the performance.

Leaving part of my heart with Rama, I started reading the shlokas for the yagna. As I have begun to read the slokas, some new set of energy is passing within me. The more I started chanting, the more concentrated I became. I am so immersed in my complete self that other than Rama in my heart and Lalitha Devi before me, I could not see anything or hear anyone.

"Mother, mother."

I think Kusha would have called me, but failing to respond to his call, he has just placed the flowers near me. I do not know how he managed to get these from a completely unknown place. After cleaning the flowers, I sat to worship Lalitha Devi with all my devotion. Some women in the hermitage have also come here to worship with me. But I did not find Lava anywhere nearby. I wish that Lava does not be rude to anyone, inviting unnecessary disputes in the matter of protecting the hermitage.

"Sita, are you performing this yagna, for us?"I could hear some inner voice tapping me.

"Yes, Rama. I have doubted you, and now I need to perform this yagna as a redemption for the mistake I have committed. Please bless me." I asked Rama's illusion.

"Sita, my blessings will always be with you," said Rama.

I was about to extend the conversation, but I could no more feel that Rama was near me. I have resumed my prayers. The last time I immersed myself in the prayer activities was at our wedding. Even though many years have passed, I still remember very clearly the type of festivities we had to do before our marriage, during, and even after. I felt post-marriage rituals were just too many. But we did those rituals together.

Today, I am performing the ritual by having Rama in my heart. Some portion of my heart, I left there at Ayodhya to view the most remembered event in the history-the, Ashvamedha Yagna, that Rama is performing for the goodness of humanity.

I am scared thinking about Lava, which would reduce my attention on the precious vrat that I am performing. So, without much deviation, I was hoping that Lava would be alright. Kusha, if he is there with Lava, I would not need to even think so much on this issue. Kusha is the elder brother kind where his eyes would always be to protect his younger brother, Lava. Since he has his task to be performed here, I was quite perplexed about how he could protect his brother from going into petty disputes.

Suddenly Lava came into the hut. Lava's presence was like a tremendous sense of relief. He appears to be very calm and composed. I am trying to show some sense of gesture so that he would come here and sit, but he is just looking like a protector casting his eyes somewhere. Even though he is sitting in the hall, his eyes appear to cover the entire hermitage. His eyeballs are moving so much in a quick direction that he is not just allowing me to make eye contact.

But somehow, after looking at him at different intervals, I have finally been successful in conversing with him with my eyes. "Lava, please come and sit for at least half an hour."

"Mother, I have to take care of the protection at the hermitage, as Valmiki Maharshi has suggested. I have come here to look at the condition if everything is quite alright or not. I will take your leave now, mother, and will get back to you in a while; once I ensure that the safety of this place is in control, I will get back as soon as possible. Please grant me leave, mother." Lava asked me.

I nodded my head quite firmly, indicating yes.

Lava took leave, and I resumed my ritual. The first part of the ritual is completed by invoking the blessings of Lalitha Devi and worshipping her with the specific flowers and praying for my dear Rama, family, and the people of Ayodhya,

Before beginning the second session, we started preparing all the necessary food and fruits. I am very much fascinated here at the hermitage is the work division. We, at Ayodhya, perform only activities assigned to us, and we never even get to know what others are doing. Do they need our help? What are they doing? Will they need some raw material that we can provide? We live in our own world.

Drawing an analogy between modern and village lifestyle, Ayodhya could be, without any doubt can be called a modern city, whereas Valmiki's hermitage is the rural one. Two significant differences I have noticed during my stay here and there at Ayodhya is that, at Ayodhya, it feels as if we have entered into nature's territory and occupied its place. And thence, not many birds and animals are found in sight. In contrast, Valmiki's hermitage is like one in nature and one with nature. The ascetic life is all about living in coercion with nature. It's like two completely different species living together.

Though many might not agree with me, the second difference is that I feel that the people at Ayodhya are more self-centered, and the hermitage people are broad-minded. The roles of the Ayodhyian people impose some set restrictions on them. Their duty-bound roles curtail them from performing any activity beyond. Hence they might not get any chance to outlook or outperform their duty. Like me, I at Ayodhya was not even allowed to get into the massive kitchen of our palace. I wish to cook my husband Rama with the recipes I learnt from my favorite cook at Ayodhya. But at Ayodhya, I can count the times I went to the kitchen and made something, and it's just at my fingertips. But, when we went to the vanavas, the bond with nature grew; secondly, I started to cook food and serve Rama and Lakshmana. There is some joy that comes along when your husband tastes the dish you have prepared and says you have done it very well. Beyond this, the satisfaction they receive from having the dish by their wives is immense.

"Sita, the delicious taste of the dish you cooked makes me completely dumb. I am restricting my speaking because I need the taste to be imprisoned inside me. I need it completely for myself. I won't let any part of the taste escape from any outlet, for that matter. I need to go now, but your taste makes me drowsy. It feels like I would go into some long slumber… Please, thence, do not delicious food."

When I was thinking about food, I got reminded of Rama's words. So where was I, yes here at the hermitage, today while I started to cook the prashad to the goddess, we have to put so much variety food, I then thought, I will have to make it fast and get it done before the auspicious time completes. As I started cooking, many people, near and dear, came to help me. I said, "Thank you so much for your help. But I can do it. You, please carry on with the works."

"Mother, Loka Pavani. It's our pleasure to help you in this ritual you are performing. Please allow us. Perhaps, sharing is caring. The more we share the tasks, the more joy we get", said the neighbour.

I could not say no to them. So, they divided the tasks in an orderly manner, which shocked me. Their management skills amazed me.

In between carrying out our tasks, we also had a great time. These women sang several songs, which kept us engaging. I have never felt this enthusiastic about cooking. I had not even imagined that cooking in a group would be this much fun. While we spent our time together cooking, our bond has also grown. We started discussing from the events in our hermitage to the yagnas that nearby hermitages are performing. The discussion that I never wanted to happen between us has come. About Ayodhya. Even though it has been nearly fifteen years since Rama abandoned me, the debate seems fresh about me, Sita.

"Loka Pavani, I think you would have known about Rama, the King of Ayodhya who is responsible for the cruel banishment of his wife, Sita."

"No, I do not know. I have just heard about it", said I.

"And the most gruesome of all is that he has banished Sita while she was pregnant. The most distressing news is that we all do not know if Sita, after banishment, is still alive or not. It seems nobody knows or has heard about her."

"Yes," I replied by nodding. "All we can do is hope she could be alive in some place on this vast planet, and she would be happy with her newfound freedom."

I have very well noticed the change within myself when whosoever talks about the case of banishment; I once used to fall sick and would take some time to regain consciousness. Even though there is such a deep discussion concerning Sita and Rama, I have replied aptly, and the debate on banishment is no more hurting me.

From Ayodhya, the discussion has come back to the hermitage. Women again started to discuss hermitage, their children, their education, etc. After two hours of cooking and discussing, we have everything served before the goddess.

With the suggestions from the sages on the chapters to chant, I have started performing the vrat. I have also sent the message to the kids about the lunch. I have seen them only in the morning and have not even found them later. This is how I find them as dedicated as their father. They were on fast today morning, yet it seems absurd that they are not hungry till now. Hoping they would come and eat, I started chanting.

***

When I started, I could hear both the brothers had come for their mid-day meal. I took a deep breath as I found some extra peace to start the event. After hours of chanting and prayers, the first day of the nine-day vrat has ended. I just went outside to take a deep breath and found nature peaceful. Actually, on a lower note, my throat has started paining. It might be due to the relentless hours of composition. Now I understand how difficult it could have been for Lava and Kusha actually to learn the entire singing composition and sing. It's been a very long since I chanted. As I have already mentioned, it was some years ago during our wedding. I should practice it regularly from now on.

I can see Lava and Kusha coming quickly, as fast as they could, in some distance.

"Mother…mother…mother…"

"Haven't you seen how peaceful the hermitage is today? Have you felt any sense of discomfort today?" Before I could even answer…

"No, you would not have felt it because it's your son who has protected you all today. I am a good protector. Isn't it?" By the time I could answer again,

"You all would have been happy. Happiness is what matters to a protector."

By the kind of expectations that Lava has, he behaves like a ruler and looks like he is taking feedback from his citizens after the one-day rule. Before asking if we are satisfied or not, he seems genuinely happy today.

Kusha looks so exhausted. He came immediately and said, "Mother, if you can provide my dinner early today, it would be so sweet of you. I need to sleep early today."

Lava also comprehended, "Yes, mother, I am also starving. Besides that, I feel so very exhausted. I need a good night's sleep to rejuvenate for the ongoing duty as a protector. But, mother, I must say this to you. When Valmiki Maharshi chose this role for me to safeguard the public, I felt very excited and was dancing in joy. Today, once I started the task, I realized how hard it is to maintain peace. If anyone uttered a word against my brother or me, I would be in a rage and throw arrows without even giving a second thought. For me, the present matters the most. When I was a kid, mother, you warned me so many times to go for peace than violence and embrace your enemy with your words. I did not understand at that point, mother. Today, there was a petty feud going on between two little boys.

He continued, "They were fighting for some ridiculous reason, mother. When I asked them to explain, it made me laugh a lot. But then again, I have tried a lot to make a peace treaty between them. Even you would have felt the same when I said about such petty disputes. Isn't it? Looking at Lava and placing my hand on his shoulders, I smiled.

"Looking at this silly argument, I felt how insanely childish I was. I have indulged in so many petty disputes like this mother. And, mother, beyond this, I have also understood one thing which you used to say always. But only today, when I have experienced it, do I understand why you repeated the same phrase. Avoid war, and promote peace. But I used to take it lightly. Today, while I tried to solve it, I understood how hard it is to maintain peace."

I was about to stop Lava from being so much philosophical. I have never seen this dimension of him. Not to suppress the expression of feelings at once, I have tried to do it through gestures, but he is not paying any attention to me and is still narrating today's story.

"Lava, you are already so tired today. Just take some rest. Let's have a quick dinner and sleep. You have your safeguarding duty tomorrow as well. You have done a good job today, and you have to do a better one tomorrow", I said.

We started to go for dinner. I still have some cooking portions left. I then hurriedly went to cook them some delicious meal.

"Lava and Kusha, can you please wait for some time? I will take little time to cook."

"Why not, mother? We will be playing right here, outside. Please call us once you prepare food for us", answered Lava and ran towards the other balcony.

Knowing they would leave the premises, I warned, "If you both cross our home and go out to play, remember, there would be no dinner for you." Seeing they had already started to go away from me, I shouted as much as possible. But I do not think they would have heard as there was no reply. I quickly prepared the dinner and served it. Lava, with an innocent face, "Mother, will you please feed me today." Just Lava's look is enough to convince me. I do not even need him to ask for it. Kusha is still sitting with his leaf in front of him. I understand that he would not have asked, understanding my situation.

"Come, let me feed you both. Wash your hands and legs and come. Also, grab the drinking water jug on your way", I said.

After dinner, I have sung them a sweet melody song and quickly put them to sleep. I have to make a few arrangements for tomorrow. Let me make that fast and sleep.

After finishing the preparations, I was doing all the preparations in half-slumber mode. I was not actually having any consciousness while I was performing those tasks. Quickly finishing my before-sleep prayer rituals, I went to sleep after such a long day.

I should say two things to reflect on how the ritual went today. Firstly, I got used to the chants and slokas; chanting them was quite a difficult task on the first day, but today I found it better to chant, and hence I felt that the ritual session had completed a bit quicker today.

Secondly, the first day would be a bit difficult if you have a ritual for a week or so. Even before the first day starts, we would be put into some tension, and even though things are easy to manage, we actually quite end up doing in a hurry. I hope you all agree with this. Today, the second day, my mind has been used to the ritual, making it a bit easy task. And above all, the thoughts about my children, if they had lunch, did not bother me much today.

Today, everything seems to have gone well. The weather looks pleasant. I am in a good mood. Hence I might be finding the weather good, and I do not know. I have even done the cooking session quickly today. Everything seems to have been preponed for an hour.

I have even wrapped up today's session even more quickly. I also found some extra time to sleep after many days. I have put Lava and Kusha to sleep by narrating a beautiful story by patting their back. Lava and Kusha, these days, are getting back to sleep even before finishing the quarter of the story. The more tired they are, the quicker they fall asleep.

Doing the daily routine, by spending some extra time in prayer, I have gone to sleep.

***"

Sita! Sita!" I felt as if someone had knocked on the door. I have opened it. Much to my surprise, it is the one who would have never expected to visit this hermitage. How did he come to know that I live here? The second I saw him there, I just felt surreal. I have even cross-checked by pinching myself to see if it's a dream. But deep down in my heart, I do not want it to be a dream. Why did Rama come all at once, out of nowhere? There was neither conversation nor some point of contact to share the information. But today, I see Rama right in front of my eyes. Before Rama could even utter a word, I quickly ensured that no one was watching us. It was still very dark. With the alignment of the stars and the moon, I think it would be too early in the morning. In summers, the brightness peeps into the world a bit early. Since it is at the peak of the winter, there is no sense of light anywhere around.

I quickly stepped out of the house and wished Rama. "My Rama, my dear husband, Did it take these many years to come to me? But, even after these very long and challenging years, I still have one question circulating in my mind. I prefer saying, in my heart. Even though it was initially tough to hear the news that you had abandoned me, I took my time and found solace within myself and in myself. When the people of Ayodhya doubted my chastity, sending me without even saying a word and getting to know the news from others was quite absurd. Maybe that is why, when I have come to take your blessings in the morning, you have acted well. Every day I find you awake when I come to take morning blessings. But, that day, you have shown no signs of movement."

By holding my hands and looking straight into my eyes, Rama said, "Sita, first calm down. I am here to answer your every question. I understand how tough it would have been for you to hear about the abandonment. Right after you asked my permission to take you to the vanavas to seek blessings from the rishis, I heard the most poisonous news. My heart broke after hearing such information, and I could not digest it. I did not know what to do. You know how venom like these spreads at Ayodhya. Even faster than the wildfire and, if I could say, even more fierce. After going through such a hard time at the vanavas and killing the demon, Ravana, people know very well how challenging the situations would have been, but still, they have questioned. And this would go on and on. Leaving their ability to themselves, the one thing that was heart-wrenching the most was the blame upon you.

They have not even witnessed the great trial by fire that you have gone through. It was just amidst a few people. But you know, Sita, that good does not spread as quickly and faster as evil does. There is one saying that a lie can travel halfway around the world before the truth puts on its shoes. After much speculation, I have decided to give up the throne. I asked my brothers to take kingship, but none agreed. In the critical situation of not knowing what to do, I have decided to distance you from these baseless allegations. I have strictly convinced myself that I should not let you know from my mouth. Because Sita, I cannot reveal this harsh truth to a person like you. I cannot look into your lotus-like eyes and banish you."

Tears started rolling down from Rama's eyes. It was agonizing to see such a sight in front of me. It's not fair on my part to leave a person who has come to see me teary-eyed. Garnering immense courage, I asked, "Rama, how are you doing? How is Ayodhya?"

"Firstly, Ayodhya is good, and people are also doing good. But ever since you have left Ayodhya, natural disasters are paving their route to Ayodhya in some form or the other. Sometimes, there is a massive flood, and at other times, a drought. People have come to me one day and begged their pardon. Rama, I think Sita Mata is furious with us; hence, the havoc started falling upon Ayodhya after the banishment. Please bring back our queen and let Ayodhya prosper. We have committed the greatest mistake that no citizens would have made.

But Sita, I have not come here again just because people have asked to get you back. But I have come here to ask your forgiveness for the blame we put upon you. Please forgive us and come with me. I promise that I will look after you well."

Rama stretched his hand and asked me to join him. I was in a dilemma if I should go with him, as I had already promised my mother Bhudevi that I would get back to her, and secondly, I had pre-decided to make my sons ready and hand them over to Rama. What would be their reaction if they learnt that their mother left them, but why did not even

Rama ask me about his kids? Did he even forget that I was carrying when I was banished? My mind is coaxed with many unnecessary thoughts that are just bombarding my mind right now.

Rama is still waiting for my reply, and I am still in a speculative position, in a perplexed state. Should I or should I not? I have started to think of the various consequences that follow the decision I take now. If I follow Rama now, yes, he has asked me for an apology. But is there any guarantee that the citizens would not again doubt my chastity? Will Rama give me that guarantee? No, how can he presume the situation? Nearly impossible. What would be the future of my children? They were already convinced their father would come one day and stay with them. What answer will I be able to provide them?

On the other hand, If I do not accept Rama's invitation to Ayodhya, firstly, Rama would be sad, and beyond that, life would go as normal as it was before. I could even keep up my mother's promise and can safely hand over my kids to Rama. They would also be happy to know that Rama is their father. As Rama said just now, Ayodhya is still suffering from continuous destruction in one form or the other. I have heard some sages say that if some goddess strongly feels that a great level of injustice has been done, she would show her anger in the form of greater havoc. But who would have created this havoc in my Ayodhya? Who would have been deeply angered with my banishment? As I was thinking, a similar kind of deconstruction came to my mind. I have experienced it myself. But where? Who? I thought about it for a minute. Yes, now I understand the person behind Ayodhya's destructive happenings. It's my mother, Bhudevi. That day itself, I asked my mother to stop. It was such a heavy wind blow that I bet even Rama's throne back at Ayodhya would have fallen due to the heavy winds. But then, my mother agreed to stop, and she halted it. I think she is still unhappy with the treatment I am going through and is creating havoc.

At that very instant, I should pray and convince my mother to stop the interruptive havoc upon Ayodhya. I should tell her that I still stand on my word. Unable to say this, how will I deny Rama's hand now? What reason will he even think I have to reject his proposal? After this, will he even forgive me and see me again at least once in his life? I think this would be a firm no, and Rama would not wish to see me again. But I should definitely tell him today or at any point in the future. I should live up to my word.

I have stretched my hand to turn down Rama's invitation, as I cannot tell him by seeing his peaceful and ever curious eyes. I have extended to touch his hand, but the more I extend, the farther the hand is going. What's happening? I clearly do not understand. Rama, who was right before me for more than an hour, is now trying to run away from me. But why is he doing it? Did he understand that I would not come with him through my eyes or facial gestures? People say that when I think about something, it becomes easy for people to understand what I am thinking.

Maybe it's because, while I am thinking, I unconsciously display my thoughts on my face. But why is Rama running as fast as he could? Is he not even concerned about listening to my reply? What could be the scenario? I can sense that someone is touching my back, calling me. Did Rama come back again? Did my Rama come back again? With so much excitement, I turned around to see him, but suddenly, my eyes were blurred. I tried rubbing my eyes for clear vision with the help of my fist; yes, the image is getting better now. I can now see a person standing in front of me. Smiling as much as I could, I looked at him, but... the person was Lava.

"Mother, what happened to you? Are you alright? I have been trying to wake you up for an hour, but you are still blabbering something and have just extended your hand like this. Lava touched my throat and hands to check if I was feeling feverish. No, mother, you are alright. But have you not just checked the time? It's early morning, and you must prepare for day three of the ritual. I am ready and waiting for my brother to come so that we would perform our duties."

***

I was at once aback by seeing Lava. What has happened to me till now? So, Rama's meet, forgiveness, and invite is this all a part of the dream? Uncontrollable tears fell from my eyes. I could not stop. How will I control it? By the way, why did I get such a dream at the very outset? Beyond all of this, I need to know if my nonsense blabber made any sense to Lava. If Lava understood anything, he would ask me the very instant I woke up. Lava can be rightly called the personification of frankness.

I could feel a slight headache, but I cannot narrate to you completely what has happened. I think I have forgotten; I can only remember that Rama has come and asked me to return to Ayodhya. I cannot even recall what my answer was. Even in my wildest dreams, I do not want to hurt Rama or speak harshly.

"Mother, please make the proper arrangements and be ready; I will get you fresh lotuses for the ritual. I have little time left by the time all the near and dear summon." But I should say, the presence of Rama in my dreams has given me some other kind of energy. I finished all the preparations in an hour. Usually, I would take a minimum of two hours to prepare everything. As I sat to chant, Kusha came and handed over the flowers timely.

I could see many women arriving with flowers and coconuts. Soon the hall is filled. But while I was chanting, some inner conscience inside me started to tap. "Sita, Sita, you have forgotten to pray."

What, impossible! I have done the usual prayer that I regularly do. There would not be anything that I would have missed. What is that? Suddenly my head started dragging. Some extreme pain behind. Sita, please pray to your mother to cool down. She is creating a kind of havoc there when she is sad or worried about you. At once, I prayed to my mother goddess Bhudevi to cool down.

***

"Mother, please cool down. I know you are dissatisfied with the amount of injustice meted out to your daughter. Please forget the past. Forgive Rama and the people of Ayodhya. I am happy now performing the yagna, the reason you would have known. As I said, mother, I will keep up your promise. Lava and Kusha, I have almost made them in the image of their father. Now, the only task left is 'Time,' the greatest force and the reigning champion. As said, 'Time and tide wait for none'; I am just waiting for the perfect time for their reunion. And with this, I would be happily ever after in your eternal realm", I pleaded.

"Sita, I understand the intention behind your worship. But think, whose mother on earth would be happy if their daughter faces endless difficulties? Firstly, will you be happy if your son faces a small difficulty or trouble? Definitely, not. Likewise, how would I feel when my daughter, who has been brought up very well by King Janak and Queen Sunaina, is married splendidly, after marrying Rama, she first followed her husband to the forest. There she faced innumerable troubles, and later on, she was abducted by the demon Ravana. All of this is fine; as a wife, I agree it is one's duty to be with their husband."

She continued, "Even after such a forceful abduction and challenging time at Lanka, after the war, Rama says, I have protected you because it is my duty as a king. You can now go where ever you want. How on earth can a wife bear such a disgrace? Even beyond this, when the coronation happened, and everything is well and fine, just because some countryman in the corner uttered something ill, Rama has banished you permanently to the forest. How do you think, Sita, that I would be happy? You were banished when you were pregnant. How much injustice is this on Rama's part as a husband?

When you have asked me to stop the horrific wind that day, I have halted it.. Now, whenever I feel a profound sorrow upon you, every time I get reminded of you, I would again, by invoking my powers, raise winds, floods, or create a drought. Ayodhya was never a lively place after you have been banished, Sita."

"Mother, Bhumata, I can completely understand the sadness behind your rage. Just for me, do not let the people of Ayodhya suffer."

"This is the reason you are hailed as Sita. Such a pure soul you have. Just because you have requested me, I am accepting. Even Rama is performing Ashwamedha yagna for the prosperity of Ayodhya."

Before I could reply, my mother had taken my leave. She has vanished somewhere deep inside in the wink of my eye.

***

The third day of the ritual was a kind of roller coaster journey. But today, I decided I should sleep as early as possible.

"Lava, without even going for a bath, what are you doing here under the tree?" I asked.

"Mother, the arrows Valmiki Maharshi gave me sharp arrows, and they need the flexibility to throw them. The bow has become outdated and needs a bit big and a flexible string. Hence you find me here, under this tree, trying to find the right bow. And I have to shape it accordingly, mother."

"Good Lava. Finish it off soon and come for the pooja ceremony. And where is Kusha?"

"Kusha has already gone to collect the flowers. He would be already on his way back home, mother."

After cleaning the pooja space and lightening the lamps, we sat together to perform the pooja.

"Mother, Kusha has sent these flowers to you." Kusha's friend handed over flowers to me.

"Where is Kusha?" I asked him.

"He is coming behind with some more flowers, mother."

Everything went sound and reasonable today. But after some time, I could feel something was not good. There might be some trouble with my dear ones, Lava and Kusha, somewhere. With this sudden drilling of thought in my mind, I cannot concentrate. When this turns up, I got reminded of Valmiki Maharshi's words. Unable to contain myself, I have called one of Lava's   friends   to   enquire aboutLava.

"Do you know where Lava is? Have you seen him?" I asked.

"Yes, Mother, I have seen him with his group. They headed somewhere towards the east", he said.

"But, why did they even go in that direction? Anyways, please call him as soon as possible." I asked him.

"Sure, Loka Pavani Mata. Will do the needful." He left.

I cannot contain myself until I get to know about Lava. My intuitions never went wrong except once. Oh, goddess Lalithamma! Please help Lava. I would have gone searching for him, but I am bound to perform this ritual. I have also been strictly advised not to stop it in between. But, putting up my concentration in the vrat and performing is becoming tough. It's as if I placed two rollable objects on my head and tried to balance them. I could not chant for some time, but again, by regaining my strength from inside, I resumed.

"Listen, Sita! You know how much important it is for you to perform this yagna. If you pause this, you won't be able to get another chance to perform such a divine act. Just recall your struggle with the pain of doubting your dear Rama and how much courage and strength were involved in asking Valmiki Maharshi the act of redemption. You are already halfway through, and you need to stay calm. Lava and Kusha are giving their maximum to help you in the vrat. You know, it is hard to collect flowers from the nearby mountains, but still, Kusha is undertaking huge adventures every day; for whom? For you. And this ritual is also for the well-being of not just Rama and the people of Ayodhya but your kids as well. Remember all this.

And beyond all of these, know who you are. Never have you before stopped any act, in the middle, abruptly. When you were a kid only, you would not let your father, King Janak, stop the story in between. You have waited very much patiently for your man in the Swayamvar. The procession did not take hours or days, but it took some months, and you have waited so long for it. Did you give a break for the procession, as it's taking unusual time than expected? No. And while staying in the forests, following the banishment of Lord Rama, do not you remember how long you used to wait for Rama's return? Have you given up? No. And after the abduction by Ravana; in the unknown land, unknown people, unknown destiny, Ravana has tempted you with so many jewels and wealth, the status of the queen, yet you have not succumbed to his advances. Did you give up your courage to live there? No. When you have been banished to the forests without your mistake, you were on the verge of taking your own life, but did you? No. Why, because you are Sita. You possess the immense strength to control your mind, Sita. Bring that out."

But, when I did all of the things that you have just mentioned, it was just for me. It was for myself. But now, I have my son on the other hand. Any mother would even sacrifice her own life and try to protect her sons. Is it not? You mothers, I think you would agree with me.

The inner conscience woke up again, "I completely understand, Sita, but have some patience is what I am asking. You have asked one of Lava's friends to search. You are still not clear about what has happened and what is happening. So, wait and let the boy come. Do not deviate."

My inner self appears to be stronger than my own. It has completely dominated my thinking process and has, in one way, ruled over me. After this huge speech, I do not even want to think about Lava. I am leaving it to God's hands, and He should take care of Lava and Kusha, who are yet to come. I am not worried because Lava is somewhere; even before confirming his actual situation, I worried about my overthinking.

Back to the ritual, I kept my ears as alert as possible to know if the boy I enquired about Lava would come and give me any information. I have finished the first session, and we have come together to cook the meals.

In one of the meals, I added rock salt instead of jaggery. I did not realize this unless one of my neighbouring women noticed.

"Mother, Loka Pavani. What happened to you? Are you feeling better? So far, you are always conscious of any activity that you perform. But today, you have added rock salt instead of jaggery. Please listen to us. Go rest and come back for the afternoon session", advised a neighboring woman.

"No, I am alright. Just feeling a little dizzy due to the fast. Once we put the items for goddess Lalitha Devi, I can eat."

"Yes, we get your point. But do not overstress yourself. If you need any help in the mornings, inform us, and we will be there," said neighbours.

This is the broad-mindedness I was talking about, the difference between people here and at Ayodhya. You can witness the amount of respect they show towards one another. I am not judging the situation in Ayodhya. I should not as well, and I am just commenting; my heart grieved when the superiors over there looked down on servant Mantara. More than a servant, she has become a mother to Kaikeyi. Irrespective of that fact, new people coming to Ayodhya still comment on her ugliness and posture. Sometimes, they even laugh at her. But the strength of the servant Mantara lies not in her beauty but her inner self. Such bullying I have not noticed here. People are always happy to help each other and share their joys and sorrows.

And now we are ready for the food offering to goddess Lalitha Devi. All I have left now is the hope that Lava and Kusha would at least return for lunch, as they have been doing earlier. While I was completely immersed in singing devotion in praise of goddess Lalitha Devi, I grasped that some kid was running towards us through my alerted ears. At once, I looked behind.

Yes, he is coming. The kid whom I have sent to enquire is coming. I tried to guess the result through the facial expressions that he made. I cannot look at his face as he is coming from far away. I then waited patiently for his reply.

"Mother, as you said, I have enquired about Lava. Something is wrong", said he.

"What happened?" I screamed out of pain.

"This is what the three friends who stay with Lava have told me," he said.

***

As a group, we were performing the guarding duties at the end of the hermitage, the border where we have a tall palm tree. We heard the footsteps of some group of people, walking unanimously; we could even make out the horse noises.

The nearer they came, we could hear that they were shouting something. As they approached a little near, we understood that it was "Ashvamedha Yagna Jayam Jayam." The three friends have seen something strange and came rushing to Lava.

"Lava, Lava. It's coming. It's coming. It's coming to our hermitage."

"What is coming? Why are you scared? Why are you even shivering?"

"Lion, lion is coming."

"When we went to collect grass for our little deer. We saw the lion. And we started running, as fast as we could. While we looked back at it, we saw the lion eating grass."

"What? Lion eating grass? Impossible, actually have you ever seen a lion" asked Lava.

"Though we have not seen it, we often heard about it when you and your brother used to talk about it. It also has a long mane. The tail is also as long as a broomstick. Do you think that we do not know? The color of it is also so very fair. It has horns."

"No, not horns. They are ears", corrected others. But the young friend shouted, "Ears will be long, but not on the head."

As in when they were discussing, the figure they have been talking about has come close.

"Here it is, see. That is not the lion, you people. It is a horse. I have also seen that in Ayodhya", said Lava by going near the horse.

While they three stayed behind, Lava alone went towards it. There is something written on the head of the horse, on a golden plate, and Lava started reading it.

"Oh! My goodness, It is the horse sent by Sree Rama. Please leave it, Lava."

"No, I won't leave. Neither the horse nor the brilliant opportunity that I have got today", said Lava.

"Lava, we have learnt about Sree Rama in the teaching that he is the saviour of dharma, right", reminded one of his friends.

"Oh ho. Just like the farthest mountains, which appear smooth, what do you people know about Sree Rama? Nothing. When we went to Ayodhya, we saw Rama with our own naked eyes and heard about his qualities through our ears. You listen, how good is Janaki Devi? She is very virtuous and Lokamatha. To such a virtuous woman like Janaki Devi, Rama that you all praise for his dharma, he had banished her to the forests", Lava said.

When the kid is narrating the events that happened there and tears are getting uncontrollable. It seems Lava's rage against Sree Rama has still not decreased.

"That too, when Rama banished her, she was pregnant. And we know how perilous it is to stay in forests and what if some animal has killed her?

We are chanting Rama's name only because I am scared of my mother. Otherwise, my brother and I do not like to chant. He also always says that he is the son of a brave mother. Are we not sons of our courageous mother? Even I know astras." Lava told.

"But you all have to do one favor. Never tell my mother I have caught this horse", Lava requested his friends.

They have then promised that they would never talk about this even if it is at the stake of their own lives.

And then, as expected, Rama's army personnel came and shouted, "Which wicked crook tied this horse?"

Lava, with so much confidence, "Mind you, tongue man, I have tied the horse."

The army personnel could not believe that a young lad like Lava could do this, and with an exclamation, he shouted, "You did this! Do you think this is a childish game?"

Lava, with ever more intensity, "No, I have not thought of them as childish games, but elderly games with animals like you."

"You kid, this is Sree Rama's yagna horse."

Mother Loka Pavani, this argument went beyond what one could expect. Lava's three friends have started sarcastically replying to those soldiers. "Everything is written on its face: the information about the horse, what is it, from where it has come, and why has it come. You do not need to tell us about that."

The army personnel became very serious and warned, "If you do not leave the horse, we will break your skull like a watermelon. Mind it."

Lava's friends, as a retort, started making goat's noise. As a reaction to it, the soldier took out his sword. At once, Lava drove his sharp arrow and cut the sword. The three friends laughed heavily, to which he drew an enormous sword and pointed it towards them. With so much vexation, Lava quickly shot his arrow and cut the sword for the second time. With this, the entire army that started this dispute ran away.

Lava should not have been in such a clash, I thought helplessly. No wonder they called their leader Shatrughna and took him away. Putting an end to my thoughts, I asked the boy, "What happened next? Is this the reason behind taking Lava?"

"No, mother, this is just a beginning; much more has happened beyond this. Shatrughna arrived and asked with much fury, "Who has tied the horse? Oh boy! It's you, right."

"Yes, I have tied it. It's written to catch it if you are a daring one. I am that daring. Are You?" said Lava.

"Why do I not appear like that? Age is not a factor to consider a daring and dashing personality", said Lava with more courage.

"Do not you know how many daring and courageous acts Rama did?" questioned Shatrughna.

"I think you are now aware that Sree Rama is the one performing the yagna, and this horse belongs to the Sree Rama," stressed Shatrughna.

"Oh, greatness, excellent then. Only when I get into a duel with such a daring person can we also prove our daring attitude", said Lava.

"Then, go ahead. Show your courageous attitude. I have shown pity upon you, thinking you are a kid. But your behavior is quite annoying, and you are just speaking beyond your age. Now will you leave the horse or not?" demanded Shatrughna.

"I won't leave it with just a verbal war. If you can, try to release it", said Lava.

"I won't leave you, kid", said Shatrughna.

Lava enthusiastically replied, "Come on, come on, if we get into a fight here, the arrows might hurt the horse. Let's go a bit far." Lava seemed very much ready to face the defiant Shatrughna.

My heart became quite unstable when I heard that he was getting ready for the war with his uncle. What is happening there? Even in my wildest dreams, I never thought that this day would come too soon.

"Mother! Lava on one side, followed by Shatrughna on the other hand. While the entire army stood behind Shatrughna, Lava just stood alone fearlessly. They both are ready with their distinct arrows. Lava started using some astra and began the fight with his first arrow. Shatrughna also released an arrow from his side.

As the people were witnessing Lava's single arrow multiply as it was travelling through the sky, even Shatrughna's arrow started multiplying; both the sets of arrows led to a horrific collision and collapsed onto the ground.

Lava then released his second arrow, to which Shatrughna, with great power, released his arrow. When the two arrows were in the air, some smoke evolved out of Shatrughna's arrow, making Lava fall unconscious. The Shatrughna's army was very happy with Lava's defeat.

But Shatrughna, with some anguish on his face, rushed towards Lava.

Stratrughna, looking at Lava, started praising him. Asked his associates, do you think he is the son of a Brahmin?

"Maharaja, even though he looks like the son of a brahmin because of the attire, he seriously has that rock kshatriya heart", said, soldiers.

"Because of fate, I have committed to such an act. I should show this kid to brother Sree Rama", said Shatrughna.

Then they released the horse, took Lava in the chariot, and left the place.

Hearing this, unable to hide my tears inside, I gave a loud shout expressing all my sorrow. The young kid was horrified and ran away.

***

"Lalitha Devi, Jaganmatha, even you are a mother, I hope you can comprehend my pain. Away from my husband, in the forests, I have been living for my two kids; if you even take them away from me, why should I live, mother? Devi, please save my dear Lava and show some courtesy upon me until I won't leave your legs. I will be here at your feet." I cried.

"Mother! mother! Kusha came with the flowers, now", a child said.

"Mother, why are the tears in your eyes? What happened, mother? Please speak. Why are you drowned in sorrow? Please tell me, mother", asked Kusha.

"My dear son, some maharaja has defeated your brother in a war and is taking him on his chariot," I spoke.

"Mother, do not fear. I will go there at once and save Lava from that treacherous army. Please do not doubt my capability and send me at once, mother. Please bless me and send."

How can I stop Kusha from going to the rescue? Only he can do it. By blessing Kusha, I have at once sent him, equipping him with his arrow.

"Mother, now, without any thought or doubt, take these flowers and perform the pooja, and for getting the prashad, I will be here soon along with my brother", said Kusha and left fast.

I have resumed my deeksha. Innumerable thoughts started striking my brain back and forth. Because of Valmiki's advice, I am able to concentrate and continue my deeksha for these many days, especially today in such a disturbing situation as well. I am not able to let my mind and heart stay stable. Whom should I find fault? Lava or my dear Rama or Shatrughna. What should I even do now? Completely helpless. Again and again, my patience is getting completely distracted.

Lava has mistaken the yagna that Sree Rama is doing and wants to save the hermitage from being occupied. The mistake is also on my part; I should have told him everything about how the Ashvamedha Yagna works.

But, wait a second, why did Shatrughna take Lava away to show to Rama? Shatrughna, who thinks twice before performing any act, did not think the boy will have his mother and family waiting for him. Did not he think that he is against the conduct of war? Why am I being put to endless tests? One after the other, one after the other. Kusha is my only relief now. I know that he will save Lava from the clutches of Shatrughna, but what if they go so fast that Kusha cannot find them? No, Lalitha Devi is with me, and she does not let that happen. I should stay strong like I am always and won't even let the thought of Lava not returning enter my mind.

Fighting the thoughts with so much courage, I resumed chanting the mantras, this time with much dedication and attention. I started performing the ritual so much that even people around me were shocked. They could not even take their eyes away from me.

Ahead of the lunch hour, hunger grabbed the pain from my eyes; I started feeling so hungry as if I had not eaten for days. I served the food to everyone here, then sat to eat. You all know how I share and with whom I share my happiness and sadness. It's with nature around. I have changed my lunch place, and today, I sat in front of a huge home opening so I could experience a better view of nature. Yes, I started finding good solace in nature. Looking at the birds going to nests with food in their beaks, the deer moving in groups, the swaying of the plants, and the shade that the huge tree is offering, everything appears so appeasing to my teary eyes. In this tumultuous situation that I am in, currently, nature is my greatest support.

Even while observing nature, I have started to look beyond nature. I have begun to look beyond what nature has to offer. I am looking at the man-made path between the huge trees, and I am looking at the fence beyond the thick bushes; I am looking at the sky that shows signs way in advance.

Beyond hearing the sounds of nature, the chirping sounds of the birds, the sound of the heavy wind, and the sounds of the friendly fights between animals, I can even hear the minute sounds of fallen leaves. This reflects how attentive I am to grasp any clue about Lava and Kusha. Sitting in front of the home, I am waiting to hear the greatest sound that any mother loves to hear, "Mother."

I wish to start the next session by giving prashad to Lava and Kusha. But, wait I can hear someone running from afar. Will that sound be of Lava and Kusha? As in they came near, I could listen to that sound more and more attentively. Will they be Lava and Kusha? My heartbeat started increasing out of curiosity. I am not even letting my eyes wink, thinking, what if Lava and Kusha appear in that wink? I do not want to miss that. It feels as if all my senses have come together for their arrival.

But no, I could not believe my eyes; I started to rub them with the help of my fist to see if that was real. Yes, with much pain, there are not two people coming but three. I can guess from the style of their walk that they are not Lava and Kusha. Lava's walk is kind of bold; he walks with pride, and there is some sense of carelessness attached to it. On the other hand, Kusha walks with humility. They both are miles apart, not just in their walk or body language but also in their behavior. As you have travelled with me, you would have noticed how much they differ. As the three came near, I finally confirmed that they were Lava's three friends, the young lad who narrated the story mentioned.

As they were coming in the opposite direction in which Kusha went, they definitely would have seen Kusha. Let me ask them.

"My dear boys, have you seen Kusha on your way?" I asked out of curiosity.

"Yes, mother. We came in this direction to inform you about the same. We saw Kusha running in the opposite direction. We were finding Kusha to inform him about his brother Lava being taken away by Shatrughna and his soldiers. But just by seeing Kusha chase like a lion chasing the deer. In the lion's case, we usually see the lion chasing the deer for hunger, but Kusha was chasing with so much emotion. He did not even give us time to explain what had happened. But, without even stopping, he just asked us only one thing, which initially we took so much time to understand, as he was chasing so fast, we could not understand his language. He asked us, "Am I going in the right direction chasing the chariot?"

Before we could even speak anything, we just nodded our heads, and Kusha understood, and we saw him running even faster. Mother, we also came here to ask your forgiveness. Along with Lava, we were also present, and we were actually intensifying the conversation. We only made it worse, which has spurred Lava and Shatrughna to go for a war. And secondly, even when Lava was being taken away by Shatrughna, we could not even help. The army was mighty, Mother, so powerful that we were scared even to ask Shatrughna to stop taking Lava. Please forgive us, mother", they begged.

"You are also kids; you do not exactly know the intention behind the Ashvamedha Yagna. You did not make any mistakes. At least one of you could have informed us about what was happening so that we would have done something about it. Some lad informed me after Lava was taken away. Other than it, be patient. Let's wait for Kusha's return. And it's already too late to have lunch. You also would have been on fast today morning, so you should go as fast as you could, finish your lunch and come", I asked them.

"Alright, mother. We are taking your leave now. Let's hope for the best", they said and left.

I will not move away from here unless I see Lava and Kusha. I think this waiting does not leave me all alone. Apart from watching nature and sharing my joys and sorrows, the only thing through which I can contain my happiness and sadness is meditation. At once, I cleared all the place next to me and began meditating.

Initially, when my father started teaching meditation on the first day, I still remember, that before meditating, I was actually inquisitive to meditate. As kids, we all would be equally curious to perform any new thing, and so was I. As instructed, I closed my eyes, but after closing, I was instructed to throw away all my thoughts and focus on either a single object or leave my mind blank, but even though I had tried a lot, I was not able to do anything in the above two. Instead, I used to swing in my thoughts. But sometimes, I was even laughing out loud, getting reminded about something. Imagine laughing while meditating is such dishonor to meditation, but what can I do? My age was like that.

But as days went by, I became more and more conscious and started to meditate with concentration, much to my father's surprise. Though I was not completely dismantling the thoughts, I could sit for a stipulated period. Starting with being meditative for five minutes, my father regularly increased the meditation time as the days progressed. It was hard to meditate for twenty minutes at a stretch, but once I got accustomed to it, it helped me a lot; I could experience the change in myself. I had a more positive approach towards life; I started finding peace within myself, I started to feel happy for even small things in my life, and I was thankful and showing gratitude towards life for every second I lived. With experience, I have also learnt to be more focused, I have taken it as a challenge, and it worked.

I started with five minutes with so much force from my father; even during the age of marriage and after, I was able to meditate continuously only for two hours. But our stay at the vanavas, when Rama was away, I have been habituated to meditating for hours; I have even stopped counting on how much time I am doing it. To keep off my thoughts about Rama while in the hut, I used to meditate and would come out of the meditation mood only when Rama would call me. Sometimes, I remember he has also complained about not being in a state of consciousness. Rama usually would have called so many times, but being unresponsive, he would try to make me come out of it through touch. There were also instances when Rama used to touch me; I would at once wake up being scared. I still retain that habit. But during my stay at the Ravana Lanka, I used to meditate, trying to keep away all the unwanted thoughts, but I failed to do so because of the place I was around. Surrounded by some rakshasis and completely unknown people, how would I even like to close my eyes for a while? Impossible. I do not even want a person like Ravana actually to touch me. But I have developed to meditate by keeping myself conscious of the people around me. It was a bit difficult because after spending years abstaining from thoughts, I have been forced to be conscious, and I cannot get past it even now. As people say, it is easy to drive yourself towards a bad habit, but it takes a lot of time to get habituated to a good thing, and just like destruction is easy than construction, the same scenario applies to me.

Now, I thought only meditation could provide me with the mental peace that was not in my hands since afternoon after the young lad conveyed this worrying news. Today, before starting to meditate, I am not clear about one thing, can I be able to block all the thoughts like I have been doing for years, or will I again follow the meditation technique that I have done in the past year?

Even when I have started to think about the meditation procedure to follow, I cannot close my eyes. I tried very harder; I just could not. All I want is the sight of Lava and Kusha returning safely. Everything seems very hypothetical to answer now. Firstly, I do not know if Kusha would have successfully saved Lava, and secondly, if Lava was not saved, they would definitely carry poor Kusha with them. Thirdly, if at all this happens, Rama would try to enquire about their parents. During the Ramayana singing composition, Rama would have seen Lava and Kusha; now, after getting to know through Shatrughna that Lava has manifested the arrows very well, no doubt, Rama would doubt as to how the sons of a rishi, the brahmins can be trained in the warfare. And for sure, if asked to show their parents, Lava and Kusha would get Rama to the ashram and show me. Amidst all of this, how would I even try to close my eyes? I am not aware of what is to happen.

Hello, Sita. My inner voice awoke. "Listen, leave all the thoughts and meditate. You have meditated in worse situations than these, so meditate. I have not come to lecture you for long hours this time but to ask you to meditate, and everything would go well. Be optimistic and meditate."

I did not want to let my inner voice suggest to me beyond this. So, I have just started meditating without thinking for a minute. At once, as I started, I felt so good meditating; to be back on the lost track. I do not know how much time I have meditated or did I meditate with full concentration anyways; all of this falls short of Lava's call. I might be in a deep meditative state, but his call immediately took me out of the trance.

As soon as he came, at once, I ran to check if Lava and Kusha were fine or injured.

"Mother, we know you are checking for the injuries, but just do not worry. First, calm down; we are safe, and nothing has happened to us. Please, give us a glass of water. We are completely exhausted." Kusha told silently.

"Lava, Kusha, just be here." I have at once run to get water to Lava and Kusha. I am as happy as I feel that I have conquered the entire world. No doubt, Lava and Kusha mean the world to me, and the feeling is eternal. I have quickly sufficed them with enough water and then took the dristi so that no evil eye would fall upon these too, Kids. Applying some kumkum on their face, "Lava and Kusha, now come inside and take blessings from Lalitha Devi."

"Yes, mother. We are coming. Let us wash our hands and legs."

"Now, take this prashad, and come, I will feed you lunch." Before, I used to ask Lava at once if he had done any mischievous activity like this. But these days, I am just refraining from asking them the moment they have come. I realized that it would affect their psyche and remained silent.

"Mother, what happened to you?" asked Lava. This was an expected question from him. I was still thinking about why is he late in asking me about this.

"Lava, I am good and alright", I spoke.

"No, mother. I think you are angry with me, right?"

"No, not at all. Why would a mother be angry towards a lovable son like you", I spoke.

"Mother, when did you start hiding the truth? I have committed a big mistake today, yet you are silent", said Lava.

"Lava, you have not committed any mistake. Will you listen to your mother's words?"

"Why not, mother? Whom else would I listen to if not you?"

"Now, you cannot talk till you finish your lunch. Sit pleasantly and eat wholeheartedly, do not think about anything that has happened or will happen. Stay in the present and eat well."

"Ok, mother." Both of them nodded.

"You are not even supposed to say ok."

By smiling, Lava put his index finger on his lips and just gave a grunting sound.

"How do you eat if your index finger is on your mouth?"

Lava, with little discomfort, started to eat silently. Let them have a short nap, and then I would ask them, with peace of mind, as going for a war against Shatrughna is completely unacceptable.

***

Kusha woke up after taking a short nap.

"Kusha! What happened there? How were you able to bring back Lava." I asked.

"Mother, after chasing the chariot for a brief time, I found Shatrughna carrying Lava. It was such a vast army. I had thought enough of chasing and then decided not to run behind them but bring them to me. I used an astra, which has the power to generate fire in the middle path of their army and push to get them towards me. As expected, my astra worked, and they all have come towards me and the chariot stood right in front of me.

I went towards Shatrughna and said, "You evil soul, how dare you try to take my Lava away from me when he has got a brother like Kusha? Do you think I would let your mischievous thing happen? You are being caught. If you have hopes on your life, at once hand over my brother and the horse he has captured."

"You have misunderstood my child. I am not taking him from here for any revenge. But I am carrying him to show to my brother Sree Rama and then felicitate him in front of the court amidst everyone at Ayodhya. That's it. I do not have any problem handing over your brother to you, and you better not ask about the horse; if not, you would be in trouble", said Shatrughna.

"Trouble to you or trouble to me? Stop speaking so much. Will you give me the horse, or would you like to go for the war?" I said.

"Even after seeing your brother's condition, you have not learnt. Now, take your brother and go. But I will never give you the horse", said Shatrughna.

"Won't you give? Then, just come face it", I said.

Then, we both initiated the war. Firstly, Shatrughna released one arrow by spelling up the astra formula; I also began to spell. We both uttered the same spell, and the result, both the arrows turned into some demons, and they both started fighting. We, both were looking at them, to see who would win, but much to our surprise, we have seen, that after the rakshasas fought for some time, they collapsed.

I cast the spell for the second time and released one of the arrows. Shatrughna also released arrows from his side. Then, both the arrows turned into sharp knives, and luckily, much to my surprise, the arrow went straight upon him, and with the stroke of the knife, he fell.

Lava was still unconscious, and I sprinkled some water on him and brought him here.

"Mother, I know the mistake is on both of us." Lava came and sat on my lap. And both Lava and Kusha started communicating in some sign language.

Lava is showing the signs of no, no. He might be thinking of stopping Kusha from further narrating the story.

"Yes, mother. So please forgive us. Firstly, Lava should have gone neither for a verbal conflict nor for the war, and I should have also restrained from the war by just taking Lava back. I am extremely sorry mother."

"Yes, mother, please forgive us", replied Lava.

This time I do not have any response.

***

After they took my leave, the thought that Ayodhyian soldiers went home with a loss was completely shattering. As far as I know, the Ayodhyian army has never gone home with a defeat. This is the first time I have heard about the defeat. How would Rama react to it? How would he take this defeat? I am completely clueless. Will he come to defeat these two, as their names would have reached every nook and corner of the city, how would Rama react is the question that is bothering me right now.

While they were sleeping, I had just gone near them, and by patting their heads, I told them very slowly, "Kids, do you remember what Valmiki Maharshi has told you while teaching the astras."

After thinking for some time, Lava replied, "Mother, Valmiki Maharshi told us to use these astras carefully." Beyond that, Valmiki Maharshi has told something important.

"Yes, yes, mother. I know. Valmiki Maharshi told us never to use these astras for destruction."

"You are right. Now, what did you do?"

"Mother, please forgive us. We will try not to repeat the same thing."

"You better not. Good night."

***

I know I should not have been that harsh towards Lava and Kusha, but as I was going, Lava and Kusha were still seen murmuring between themselves. I hope they will not drag this problematic issue beyond this. Waging astras twice is the first mistake they have committed, and I do not know how Rama would retaliate to this.

Prepping up for the next ritual, I have already found Lava and Kusha are already out for their duties.

O Mother, Lalitha Devi, it feels like everything is out of control. I had never had this kind of feeling before. Lava and Kusha are hiding their feelings and many other things happening in their life. Before, when they would come to know about their dear Lord Rama performing a yagna, they would be the first persons to help Rama accomplish his mission and vision, but Lava's behaviour, I feel, has completely changed. I do not understand the reason behind it. And, as usual, Kusha would never reveal his feelings. So, it is challenging to judge Kusha. As far as I know, they have started to behave indifferently since their visit to Ayodhya, and I think they still are angry towards Rama for the act he has committed by banishing Sita. I have tried my best to explain the reality, but this issue still seems to perturb them, and I do not know or cannot guess what they would do in return if Rama came. Loka Mata, you save everybody, please, my two kids, from any mishap. Please forgive them for their notorious deeds and help them maintain peace. After being the spectator of their journey yesterday, this new prayer has been added to my list.

All I can do is sit here in the ritual and pray that nothing should happen to my dear kids. I actually would like to be with them during the tumultuous period of their lives, but I am also unable to break the limitations set up on me. Valmiki Maharshi is also not here at the much-needed time. Mother, O Lalitha Devi! I am just holding my hands and asking you again to help this poor mother again.

During the afternoon, I felt quite relaxed as Lava and Kusha had lunch at the right hour, and it looks like they had just done their duty well and had also taken a quick nap.

"Lava and Kusha, do not spend much time near the mountains, just come as soon as you both finish your work; the weather also is a bit not good as we can notice the change of the season", I said.

With so much love, they replied, "As you order, mother."

Even when we were going, I could see them planning something. Usually, even though they go together, they would actually not engage in any discussion. This is one of the major changes I am witnessing with respect to both. I saw both of them collecting something from the cow shed.

"What are you doing there, Lava? What are you collecting from the cow shed?" I asked.

Lava appears so suspicious. He is hiding something. "Lava, you have already done so many naughty things. Do not add this to your list again. Just tell me what is in your hand."

"Mother, this is grass."

"Alright. But why are you collecting grass now?

Lava appears to be pensive, "Mother, this is for the horse."

"What are you blabbering, Lava? From where did you get the horse? What horse are you talking about?

"Mother, for Rama's horse", he said.

"So, yesterday's incident, did not you give them their horse?" I seriously asked.

"No, mother. They did not take their horse. After Shatrughna fell, the entire army left at once", Kusha said.

Then, I asked in quite a sarcastic tone, "When are you planning to return their horse?"

"Mother, we would give them when they come for the horse this time."

"Do you think this is a hide-and-seek game you play? You here are playing with Ayodhya, a huge influential kingdom." I shouted.

"Mother, we did not have that intention to keep the horse with us; we will return it when they come, be it today or tomorrow", they said.

I am literally in shortage of words. I completely feel as if my mind is blocked. Capturing a yagna horse just for a few minutes is also a mistake, but this horse has been here since overnight. What can I reply to? Now, after Shatrughna, whom will Rama send for his horse? I have never even heard about an incident where the king himself would go to get back the horse.

Keeping all these aside, I have started today's ritual. I do not know what will happen, but something will happen. I then tried to put aside my deviation, and while in the middle of the prayer, I had different feelings; I felt like some sort of new breeze was touching me. I could feel some sort of mixed feelings, I am happy, and at the same time, I am sad; I am peaceful, and at the same time, I could feel some sense of calamity in my mind; I am stable, and at the same time I could feel some sense of complexity running through my mind. Why am I experiencing such mixed feelings? Again, as per my intuition, is someone going to come to take the horse? Will Rama be coming?

Sita, what will happen will happen; just focus on the ritual. I am trying to bring my consciousness back. But I could listen to some murmuring happening around me. What happened? In a word, the room is like pin-drop silence. But I could hear endless chaos happening beside me. I thought to have patience for a while and then ask all the women, part of the ritual, what had happened.

Before I thought I could open my eyes, someone uttered my name, the voice of the person very much known to me, which I have been forced not to use, but when I heard that name, I grew quite suspicious; who could that be? Does not he know not to use my actual name here at the hermitage? These days I have been trying to hide my identity, but who has revealed it at once

***

As soon as I opened my eyes, much to my surprise, I found Hanuman, a man of great strength and vigor. How did he come here? As I was unable to utter my word in shock, he spoke,

"Jaganmata, Janaki Devi, you are still alive, mother!" Hanuman asked me with more surprise.

As soon as Hanuman uttered my actual name, people around me, out of sudden shock, started, "Ah! Janaki Devi! Lord Rama's wife! Is she not a nymph? Is she Sita Devi? And the children…Lava and Kusha are Sree Rama's sons?"

The day that I have expected to come has, in fact, come very fast. I did not expect my identity to be revealed like this. How is Hanuman here? Is this the result of the war with Shatrughna yesterday? How should I react to this crisis? Firstly, I have to know what is happening around me. While I was in these thoughts, without reacting to the questions from these women around me.

Hanuman reacted, "Are those two kids the children of Sita and Rama? Yes, that is why they have already fought against Lakshman and Shatrughna, and now, they are fighting against the great Sree Rama."

Till now, I was in a silent state, unable to reply to their questions flowing from left to right. But what Hanuman has just said now is ultimately making me sick. It's even quite unpleasant to hear what Hanuman has just said.

"Are they fighting with their father? Oh, God! Why such a catastrophe?" I cried.

"Hanuma, what did you say? Is it true? Are my kids fighting against Sree Rama?" I asked.

Hanuman nodded his head. Before I could even think about what I should do next, a woman on one side said, "Mother, you should never interrupt the pooja in between; please finish the pooja and go, mother."

On the other hand, with much more intensity and rage, Hanuman said, "Mother, Lava, and Kusha have captured the horse of Sree Rama. They have defeated Lakshmana and Shatrughna as well. They have made Sree Rama itself come here."

Again, another woman, holding my hands, "Mother, if you finish this ritual, it would be good; if you stop this in the middle like this, you do not know it might lead to many unpleasant things, which you can neither predict nor imagine."

Should I comply with Hanuman's words and stop the war between father and their sons? Or should I remain here? You just imagine, after being put to all these tests so far in my life, again and again, I have been tested. If at all I go with Hanuman, what would I say with Rama, and how would I tell my kids that Rama is their father? And how would they react if Lava and Kusha knew that Rama was their father? Would they still despise Rama for abandoning their mother? They had loved Rama so much that they even sang Ramayana's composition from their hearts;

their perception completely changed after their visit to Ayodhya when they came to know about Rama's mistreatment of Sita. Or will they forget everything when they know that Rama is their father?

Above all, Lava and Kusha have been the reasons behind my survival. Their being in my womb has saved me from committing suicide. They have taken the best and worst of their times here. Challenges started right from being there in my womb and are still along with me, and because of me, they are still facing the challenges every day. While all these thoughts hit my mind, at once, the hermitage seems to appear like an actual war place. Is this the result of their ongoing war? The entire environment seems to reflect. I hear some unbearable sounds that are very heavy on my ears. We could see the trees moving heavily and more fiercely; the most unexpected things were happening, and the sky is struck with heavy thundering and lightning.

"Hanuma! what is happening? What are these sounds?" I asked Hanuman.

"What else, Mata, father-sons duel," said Hanuman.

While my heart was standing heavily inclined towards going near the war place, again, one of the women interrupted me and "Mother, do not skip the ritual."

Hanuman, with so much concern, "Sita Mata, by the time you finish this pooja, the entire world might end. Mother, please come at once and stop the war."

"Janaki Devi, if you move without finishing the ritual, it's completely unpleasant," she warned.

Already my mind is hoaxed with innumerable thoughts, and these two groups are trying to influence me in their own manner. But what exactly should I do? At this crucial time, my inner voice awoke; with a furious tone, she replied, "Look, Sita, yes, I agree that it is unpleasant to stop the ritual you have been performing for the past few days. You have not stopped it even though there have been many adversaries. I understand your grit and determination. But today, the situation is completely different, and you must proceed according to the situation. You have to move further in accordance with what life has to offer. Just tell me one thing. Why are you performing the ritual at the first stance? For whom are you performing? Before I could even think, she replied with a bigger and much stronger tone, in case you do not know, you are doing it for Lava, Kusha, Rama, and Ayodhya. Now they are all here; what else do you need in life? If you do not go and stop the duel now, you will regret it in life later. Do not have such regret and go to the battlefield at once."

My inner voice has given me enough courage to make decisions at the right time. In reply to the woman stopping me, I sternly, "What is unpleasant, and what can be more unpleasant than this? One side is my dear Rama, and the other is my two sons; even if any one of them gets hurt, where does the meaning of my life lie? Kathyayini, Lalitha Devi! Please forgive me and forgive the deed I am doing now."

"Hanuma, let's go. Please show me, my dear Rama."

Hurriedly, I went along with Hanuma from this place. When we travelled, nature was still at its height of fury. It shows even more fierce effects as we travel toward the battlefield. Now again, I am chasing my unknown destiny. I have at once stopped rewinding the past and thinking about the future. I needed to stop the battle as far as I could. I have garnered all the energy and started running to the best of my capacity and capability. I have only one thing running on in my mind. When the energy seems completely down, I will start reminding myself of the present goal to be achieved. Stop the war!

"Hanuman, how far is the place?"

"Just a few minutes, and we would be there, Sita Mata. I hope you are not exhausted, mother. Please have patience for a while", said Hanuman.

***

As we were going near, I could see in the sky how ferociously the battle between the two was going on. I could see the exchange of bows; that is astras. Both of them seem to be uncompromising. They both appear to be in a real zeal to win over the other. The weather is also changing according to the kind of astras they are using. At one point, the weather is found too much windy, the trees swinging to their maximum elasticity, the birds moving from this branch to the other, and the nests have also fallen—such a disaster. And while the wind was at its peak, all of a sudden, the weather became very still, we could not hear the noise of any bird or animal, and out of the imagination, the weather started to be rainy. It's heavily raining, restricting our movement. Finally, after following Hanuman for nearly two hours, which felt like two days, Hanuman pointed his hand in the east direction and said, "Sita Mata, look there."

Rama is standing as always with grace; the bow and arrow in his hands add even more grace. I could not believe I saw Rama with my own naked eyes. He looks the same; he is the same Rama I saw many years ago. But, even amidst the irreparable havoc, I cannot take my eyes off Rama.

"Mother, why are you standing here? Please go and stop further damage."

Hanuman's call shook me from the constant sight of looking, Rama. When I saw Rama, he drew another arrow; I needed to stop him at once. Before I could stand, I went in their direction by shouting, "How rude, how offensive, how rude, how offensive. Please stop the act at once, Lava, Kusha."

Rama has reacted. He halted, drawing the arrow at once, and touched his heart with his hand. His eyes lost focus now and are constantly looking somewhere. Did Rama understand that it was me, just by my voice? It's unbelievable, and soon he started moving hither and thither and calling my name out, "Sita, Sita, Sita!"

Yes, he found me. Our eyes met one another, and soon out of my consciousness, my hands started to come together; I folded my hands and greeted my dear Rama. I have just taken off my eyes to see what

Lava and Sita are doing; they appear to be completely unmindful of what is happening. I was shocked to see Lava and Kusha pointing toward Rama, even in this situation, and if I did not stop them now, a huge danger would occur. Rama is completely out of focus and in an unconscious emotional state now.

"Lava, Kusha, what are you doing without any sense of consciousness." I immediately took their bow and arrows from their hands and threw them down.

"What are you doing to my Sree Rama?" I shouted upon them.

"Mother, we swear, we have not done anything, mother. We were dismissing Sri Rama's Divya astras", they said.

Out of somewhere, I could hear Valmiki's voice. Is it true that he has come? Thank God he has come at the right time. Hopefully, he will assist me in this high time.

"Sita Mata, what Lava and Kusha have said is right. They have not made any mistakes. By seeing you, Rama has become quite unconscious. Please do not punish them."

Valmiki sprinkled water on Rama's face, and Rama opened his lotus-like eyes quietly.

Then, Lakshmana came to our place running and pronounced my name outrightly, "Mother, Janaki, after how many years we have seen you again, mother".

Lava and Kusha, who was still holding my feet, stood up at once and, out of excitement, "Mother, my mother is Sita Devi!" They hugged me tight, and Valmiki Maharshi said, "Yes, sons, and this great man, right in front of you, is your father, Sree Rama."

They instantly went and fell on Sree Rama's legs, no, their father's legs, and took his blessings. "Please forgive us; we have made a mistake, unknowingly. That too, we have committed the crime against our own father and made a huge mistake."

Rama, by lifting them both from their knees and hugging them together, "You have not done any sin; you have proved that you are sons greater than their own father."

Seeing them like this, both hugging Rama on either side of the shoulders, my two eyes are not enough. Tears are rolling down my eyes; this time, they are happy tears. All the difficulties I have faced so far, all the problems that I have come across, all the challenges that I have encountered, the days of endless waiting, the days of sorrow, the days of anxiety, the days of an internal duel, the days testing my patience, the days of depression, everything has vanished now.

I used to think about the past now and then and plan for our future, but this time, all the thoughts which pestered me constantly are nowhere near to me. Rama's union with his sons, this sight has now become the fence, keeping away all the thoughts.

While I am breathing, even though it is just inward flow and outward flow of air, it gives me a different feel. Along with the external flow of air, I am also releasing a huge sense of distress, and with the inward flow of the air, I am taking a huge sense of relief, and this act of breathing is now giving me a great amount of relaxation. It feels at least for this moment in life; I have to be alive. The purpose of life now seems realized. Rama is now united with his blood and flesh. Standing now here and connecting the dots behind in my life, I now understand the purpose and essence behind everything. While it was happening, I could not relate to it at all.

I always existed in some sense of confusion and constantly questioned God, the supreme power, as to why am I facing such serious issues; now, this ending has proved that God always provides us with the right thing at the right time. The love Rama had showered when I was with him and even in his absence is worth the wait. Lalitha Mata, am I being forgiven at least now? At least now, will I be accepted by Rama and the people of Ayodhya? Has that black mark on me? Has it completely gone? Only time will answer all these questions. And only through the events that are yet to happen will I know. But, why am I, or why at all, should I think of all these in the first instance? I have already faced so many troubles in life that I am neither worried about my future nor have huge expectations for it. Let me go with the flow of life. Let me witness what life has to offer for me and decide accordingly.

***

The happiness that Lava and Kusha felt as soon as they saw their father gave me enough boost to face life's challenges. How can I forget the number of days, the number of times that Lava and Kusha have asked for their father? It was even more painful when Lava and Kusha used to wake up in the middle of the night and ask me about their father's return to the hermitage. This questioning became even more intrinsic when they saw their friends spending quality time with their fathers. Only I know how hard it has been to answer their questions now, and then they ask me the number of sleepless nights I have faced due to these and the waterfall of tears I have poured down. And secondly, the pride that I see in their father's eyes is a sign that I have been right in my upbringing.

The smile of pride I see is enough to strike off all the worries I have faced alone. Life has taught me that raising a single mother is tough, but I have proved that it is not impossible. Anyways, all my worries have come to fruitification now. I can proudly go on my way whenever I want to because I have delivered a proud lineage to the Ayodhya. How happy would mother-in-law Kausalya be to know that the two naughty kids who sang the Ramayana are his grandchildren? If King Dasharath had been alive, he would have been the happiest.

"Mother, Sita Mata", called Valmiki Maharshi.

It feels completely anew when Valmiki Maharshi calls me in this manner. I grabbed my name again, trying to fly away from me.

"Mother, Sita Mata! Your ritual has finally been accomplished; now you go with Rama to Ayodhya with your children."

***

People say good times or even happy times fly faster. This is what happened in my life. It's been so long since I have spent a comfortable and quality time like this. Time flew in a flicker. While coming on the same route, I felt that nature was extremely sad like me, but this journey was all gleeful. You would have guessed already what I am talking about. Yes, the journey from the woods to my place, Ayodhya. The family is now together after so long. Everyone appeared to be good, except mother-in-law Kausalya. Right after I went inside, before I could go take the blessings by falling on her foot, she came and hugged me. Beyond this, I could see some immense light in the smile of all the people of Ayodhya. At first, they could not believe it; later on, everyone accepted that they all felt that they saw Rama's grace, and Sita's patience is found imprinted on these two.

Everything feels anew to me. Far from the ascetic life, to be back here will be different again. The entire city is celebrating our reunion. Rama called all the courtiers and asked for a very important meeting tomorrow at the Durbar. He asked the entire people of Ayodhya to be present here. He very importantly asked not even one person to be absent. When I asked why, Rama quite straightforwardly replied, "Just wait, you will get the reply tomorrow." Is it only me or is everybody finding Rama differently? He seems quite perturbed as well. He should be happy about everything that has happened so far. But he is different, is what I could say.

That night, Rama came to me and said, "Sita, tomorrow is an important day in your life. Not just in your life but also in the life and future of Ayodhya. So please, dress in the finest silk saree you have never worn and adore yourself in the most exquisite jewels. I have asked Mother-in-law Kausalya to provide you with everything. Most importantly, be as much grace as you can. I have some work regarding arrangements for tomorrow's event; I will take your leave."

"Sita!" called Kausalya. "Here is everything you should garment yourself for tomorrow's event."

"Mother, if you do not mind, shall I ask you one question?"

"Yes, Sita, there need not be any such formalities. You can ask me."

"Mother", I quite lingered. "Do you have any idea about what this event is about?"

"Sita! Rama has not said anything about tomorrow's event. He just said that it is very important. Maybe, Rama is going to sit with you along with Lava and Kusha on the royal throne, is what I could guess."

"Might be, mother. Thank You", I spoke.

I hope this will be the reason. Rama's acceptance. I hope this huge event in front of every person in Ayodhya would reduce my mother's anger. Maybe Rama would have thought that since the banishment was done privately, he wanted the entire Ayodhya to watch his acceptance. Now, I can connect why he called this an important day in my life and in the future of Ayodhya. He would have maintained it as a secret, leaving it as a surprise and making me happy. And, today I could not sleep well because not what you thought, not because I am waiting for the surprise, not about tomorrow being the big day, but my sons Lava and Kusha, who have been sleeping by my side today, are now with his father. Ever since they saw their father, they started sharing everything with Rama; it is nice to see them being happy with their father. Still, you tell me, would you get sleep if your sons who have been with you and you would sleep by telling them a story every day and suddenly, and one day they are not next to you. It's the same sense of detachment but positive, though. But just thinking of their happiness made me sleep happily. Every time I find my happiness in them and why not today?

I woke up, and at once, I remembered the mother bird, the three eggs, which obviously would have become birds, but seeing any one of the birds would mean a surprise. But unexpectedly, I saw neither birds nor the nest, which broke my heart very early in the morning. No, but it does not feel like early in the morning. I could listen to huge trumpet sounds; apart from this, I could also listen to huge sounds and cheers made by the public. The ambiance is like a festival.

"Sita, Sita", called Kausalya.

"Yes, mother, bless me", I touched her feet.

"Sita! Rama again stressed to me that I get ready as beautifully as possible. He even insisted that you get ready like the Swayamvar time."

I tried to be ready as beautiful as I could in a short period. I stood in front of the mirror and looked at myself. After how many years have you adorned yourself like this, Sita? I have started looking at myself for so long. Now, you need to go. As I started stepping out of the room, I felt the dress was a bit uncomfortable; secondly, I would be presenting myself in front of the Ayodhya Durbar hall. I was never nervous like this. I have been in the Durbar hall several times before, but why am I this tensed today? It may be because of the time gap. Sita, you are brave, and be brave said to me and entered the Durbar hall of Ayodhya.

***

The Durbar hall of Ayodhya kingdom welcomed me with tremendous cheers; children Lava and Kusa were already at the throne with Rama. The entire court is decorated so well with so many flowers, and it feels as if I am seeing so much colourful after quite a long time since Rama's coronation. I was about to sit beside Rama over the throne with my children, Lava, and Kusha. Feeling of sitting over the throne with my husband Rama and with children Lava and Kusha, how beautiful it would be? Thinking of it in mind, I hastily moved towards the throne.

Much to my surprise, Rama stopped me and said, "Sita! Please wait there for a while and listen." In front of the entire Durbar of Ayodhya, he spoke,

"O..Sita! I have two reasons behind the celebration of today's event. Firstly, in front of the entire durbar, I announce that Lava and Kusha would be the heirs to the Ayodhya throne and rule the Ayodhya kingdom." Rama said with more happiness. My happiness was of no bounds after listening to this news, and I felt enormously happy.

By seeing me, Rama said again, "But the second one is even more important than the first one, Sita! Today, amidst the entire court, I ask you to do the fire ordeal and prove your chastity so that no one in this entire kingdom would dare to point toward you again and again. You would be much revered after this act. Please prove it to the court, and then I would accept you as my dear wife."

My heart broke once again. But this time, tears did not roll out of my eyes. Rather with fire in my eyes, I lifted my head even higher. With so much confidence, I replied, "My dear Rama, is this for this test of fire that you have asked me to decorate myself graciously? That day, I have come forward to go through the test, but now go where ever you want. You have put your kingly duties first and banished me, a pregnant wife, to the forest without even a word. Now, in front of thousands of Ayodhyians, family, and most importantly, our children, you have put forward the test of fire. After these many years, the question of chastity has again come out. But this time, I am not ready to perform it. Would you guarantee that the same question of chastity would not arise again? To women out here, I would like to tell them that do not lose their self-respect. Now the time has come for me to go to my mother's lap. I have fulfilled my duty as a successful mother and have handed you the heirs of Ayodhya. Lava and Kusha, be good rulers." I said to Rama.

"O Mother, O Bhumatha! If I am pure, If I am chaste, if I have remained true to Rama in mind, please take me to your abode." I have uttered these words as loud as I can, and at once, amidst huge thunders and lightning, fierce winds, heavy rains, the floor broke, and my mother came and took me."

Rama on one side is weeping out as, "Sita! Sita! O.. Sita! O.. Sita!"

Lava and Kusha, on the other hand, are weeping, "Mother! Mother!"

I, Sita Devi, who has come from the earth, returned to the earth with pride. I have fulfilled my duty as a responsible mother to Lava and Kusha.

About the Author

Bhagya Shree Nadamala is currently a Junior Research Fellow (PhD Scholar) in the Department of Humanities and Social Sciences, Indian Institute of Technology Patna. She qualified UGC-NET JRF in English with 99.96 percentile in June 2020. She is working in the area of Gender studies, Myth and Feminism with special emphasis on the Indian Epic Ramayana.

She pursued post-graduation from the Department of English, Sri Venkateswara University, Tirupati and secured the prestigious University Gold Medal. She did her bachelor's degree in English Language and Literature from The Department of English (SFS), Madras Christian College, Chennai and won the Special Prize for topping the Department.

Her interest in writing began with penning frequent columns for The Hindu Young World Magazine in her primary school days. She puts down her thoughts in the form of poetry quite frequently. She has published three articles in prestigious journals and has attended a UGC- sponsored national conference. The prime time in Sita's life is sidelined in Valmiki's Ramayana, hence she wishes to take us through to Sita's world through her debut novel.